W9-CWK-885

motivation

>> spark initiative
>> inspire action
>> achieve your goal

Tom Gorman

BUSINESS

Adams Media
Avon, Massachusetts

Published by Adams Business, an imprint of Adams Media, an F+W Publications
Company, 57 Littlefield Street, Avon, MA 02322
www.adamsmedia.com

ISBN 10: 1-59869-091-4
ISBN 13: 978-1-59869-091-0

Printed in Canada.
J   I   H   G   F   E   D   C   B   A

Library of Congress Cataloging-in-Publication Data
Gorman, Tom.
  Motivation / Tom Gorman.
      p. cm.
  Includes index.
  ISBN-13: 978-1-59869-091-0 (pbk.)
  ISBN-10: 1-59869-091-4 (pbk.)
  1. Motivation (Psychology) I. Title.
  BF503.G674 2007
  153.8—dc22   2007018988

This publication is designed to provide accurate and authoritative information with
regard to the subject matter covered. It is sold with the understanding that the pub-
lisher is not engaged in rendering legal, accounting, or other professional advice. If
legal advice or other expert assistance is required, the services of a competent profes-
sional person should be sought.

—From a *Declaration of Principles* jointly adopted by a Committee of the American
Bar Association and a Committee of Publishers and Associations

Many of the designations used by manufacturers and sellers to distinguish their prod-
uct are claimed as trademarks. Where those designations appear in this book and
Adams Media was aware of a trademark claim, the designations have been printed
with initial capital letters.

This book is available at quantity discounts for bulk purchases.
For information, please call 1-800-289-0963.

contents

BASIC MOTIVATION

PRACTICAL MOTIVATION

iii

part

3

ADVANCED MOTIVATION

introduction

Get Moving and Keep Moving

I didn't realize it before I started writing this volume, but I'd be hard pressed to come up with a topic that's been covered more frequently in books than motivation. Every guide to success, management, self-improvement, leadership, and living at least touches upon it, and many books devote themselves solely to the topic of motivation. Every guide to managing a business, managing change, or managing yourself deals with it on some level, usually explicitly. Every book on selling tries to help salespeople stay motivated in the face of repeated rejection, while motivating their customers to buy.

Then we have the whole cottage industry—or is it a mansion industry?—of motivational speaking. Success coaches, life coaches, and sports coaches all try to motivate us. In fact, the image of the football or basketball coach delivering the motivational speech to his half-beaten team at halftime is a stock figure in sports and movies. (Perhaps the lack of halftime explains all those glum baseball managers moping around in the dugouts.)

Any topic that's caused so many trees to be ground into pulp and so many speeches to have been made must be important. When you come right down to it, nothing is more important than motivation. That's because without it you can't do anything, build anything, or be anything. Without motivation you can't even get moving. By definition, if you are doing something, pursuing something, or achieving something you are somehow motivated to do it, pursue it, or achieve it. Motivation ignites, energizes, determines, directs, and explains our behavior.

So what?

So this: If motivation drives our behavior, why are we so often motivated to do unproductive, self-sabotaging, or downright stupid things? We need to understand how we are motivated and what motivates us, at least partly because so much of our behavior seems pointless—or worse. Why do we do what we do? Why do we do things we don't want to do? Why don't we do what we really want to do? Why do we feel motivated or unmotivated?

This book answers those questions. More importantly, it shows you how to understand why you do what you do and how you can motivate yourself to do whatever you want to do. This is a guide to motivation, and a guide to motivating yourself.

Who Am I?

First, I am not a motivational speaker or guru. As a full-time, professional writer, I am a first-rate researcher and synthesizer—and a truly motivated, self-employed self-starter. I've been a successful manager, parent, spouse, and friend. And I've thought long and hard about motivation—as a student of psychology (undergraduate degree), business (graduate degree), manager, entrepreneur, and author of numerous business books.

As a writer, I have no axes to grind or products to push. Indeed, like most writers who have nothing (other than books) to sell, I am more than a bit skeptical of people with axes and products. For instance, I don't believe that "anyone can do anything"; nor do I believe that any single motivational theory, practice, book, tape, or tool can be right for everyone.

So my approach in this book is to bring you the best of motivational theory and practice, laced with my own experiences and those of people I know and people in the public eye. My goal is to show you your options for motivating yourself, and to encourage you to use them.

Note that I said encourage, rather than motivate, you to use them. I don't really believe that I can motivate you, although I may be able to inspire you. For me, inspiration is a feeling and, as with so many feelings, I've found inspiration to be a fleeting thing. It comes and it goes. But motivation stays with you because it's a decision as much as it is a feeling. You cannot achieve difficult, complex, long-term goals with inspiration alone. You need deep motivation as well. The motivated people of this world decide that they are going to achieve a goal, and they exert consistent, persistent effort until they ultimately either achieve it or fail to achieve it.

While some introspection can be useful, this is not a book for navel-gazers. It's a book for doers, and for people who want to be doers. The approach I take in this book is to explain the various theories and practices of motivation and their approaches to explaining our behavior. Then we examine various motivational practices and what various gurus say. That's Part 1. Then, in Part 2, I guide you to look at yourself and at what you really want out of life, and then to set goals that will move you in the direction you desire. In Part 3, we look at how you can sustain your motivation and how you can motivate others, and at some of the larger philosophical issues in motivation.

Great things happen in our lives when we make them happen. We need motivation to decide what great things we want to happen, and we need motivation in order to make them happen.

Let's get going.

BASIC MOTIVATION

part 1

"

THE PEOPLE WHO GET ON IN THIS WORLD
ARE THE **PEOPLE WHO GET
UP AND LOOK** FOR THE CIRCUM-
STANCES THEY WANT, AND, IF THEY CAN'T
FIND THEM, MAKE THEM.

"

—George Bernard Shaw
(playwright)

Motivation: What It Is, Why It Matters

Motivation, for our purposes, is a desire to do something that is so strong it propels you to actually do it. It's a feeling of wanting or needing something—an achievement, possession, position, location, relationship, level of health or wealth, or state of mind—so much that you take the action that you must take to achieve or obtain it.

Yes, I am saying that motivation is a desire so strong that you act on it. And I'm saying that you know you have true motivation when you act to obtain or achieve something. I know that sounds like a tautology—something that's true because it's stated in a way that must be true—but that element of action is key to motivation. If the feeling isn't strong enough to get you to act, then it's just one more want or need that you may or may not fulfill.

Simply wanting or even needing something isn't the same as being motivated to pursue it. Wants

mo·ti·va·tion

1. desire so strong that you actually act on it

2. sense that we have to do something and therefore we do it

3. feeling of energy channeled into the pursuit of a goal

and needs are too passive to be motivations. Everyone wants and needs things. Yet not everyone takes action to fulfill their wants and needs.

Motivation Is Action

Motivation, motive, movement—these words have the shared meaning of motion, doing, and action. When are you seeing motivation? What does motivation look like?

- It looks like the athlete sweating, straining, training rigorously, and competing fiercely to win a game, race, or contest.

- It looks like the entrepreneur waking up early and working late to deal with suppliers, guide employees, serve customers, and build a business.

- It looks like the student who passes up partying in favor of studying and decides to master the material rather than just pass the exam.

- It looks like parents and caregivers who put their own wants and needs aside to tend to those of their children or patients.

4

○ *It looks like anyone working to face and overcome a serious handicap, difficulty, injustice, addiction, accident, or setback.*

You'll find motivation in other forms of human endeavor too, but you get the idea. Motivation is a strong desire, a manifest desire, to accomplish something, usually something difficult. After all, if it weren't difficult, why would you need motivation?

This raises several more questions: Why is motivation an issue at all? Why do people even think about it? Sure, some things are more difficult to obtain or achieve than others. So what? You work a bit harder or longer or get help, and you get the difficult things done along with the easy things, right?

Before we answer those questions let's examine the feeling and decision aspects of motivation.

PARTS OF MOTIVATION

○ *Action*

○ *Feeling*

○ *Decision*

○ *Result*

Motivation Is a Feeling

If motivation is a desire so strong that it generates action, then there must be a feeling component, because desire is a feeling. You'll often hear people say they didn't do something because they "didn't feel like it." If they had wanted it badly enough, they would have "felt like it."

The real issue with motivation as a feeling is often one of creating and maintaining strong desire in yourself for something. Why is this necessary? If you really want something, what's the problem with motivation? Either you want it or not and the feeling's either there or not—right?

Actually, it's not that simple. This book looks at why this is so and what to do about it. Right now, I can tell you that certain aspects of the physical world and human nature work against our motivation. I'll get to these in a moment, after I get that other aspect of motivation on the table.

Motivation Is a Decision

Although motivation is an action and a feeling, if you wait to feel motivated before you Take Action, you may find yourself in a permanent state of inaction. Again, there are reasons for this, which we'll examine in the next section. However, there's a serious issue of decision—an act of the will—in motivation.

The alert reader will suspect that more tautologies, and even circular reasoning, may be afoot here. If you decide you are motivated you will feel motivated, and even if you don't feel motivated, you will be acting, and acting to achieve something is motivation.

Exactly! Here's how it breaks down. In any given instance in which you act to obtain or achieve something, a feeling (say, a craving for pizza) can prompt a decision (to order a pizza) and an action (picking up the phone and placing the order) that will create a result (the delivery man with a pizza at your door within forty-five minutes).

Feeling ▶ Decision ▶ Action ▶ Result

But what if you're on a diet? What if you've already decided that you want to lose ten pounds in six weeks and that you can't do that if you keep eating pizza? What happens when you crave pizza?

If you've really decided to lose ten pounds and you've concluded that pizza consumption will not help you achieve that result, then you decide to make a salad. You go to the kitchen; open the refrigerator, where you've stocked salad fixings; and make and eat the salad.

Why didn't you order the pizza when you craved one—that is, strongly felt that you wanted one? Because you had already decided that you would not be eating pizza and the decision overrode the feeling. Here's the relevant diagram:

Feeling ▶ Overridden By Decision ▶ Action ▶ Result

There's a lot at work in this simple diagram because a lot goes on when you want two conflicting things, such as a pizza and a trim waistline. The challenge is to use a decision to override a feeling, which isn't easy because often our emotions (feelings) trump logic (decisions). We'll explore these dynamics a bit later in this chapter. First, let's look at things that undermine our motivation.

Enemies of Motivation

Two broad types of barriers undermine our motivation and keep us from achieving things—barriers out in the world (external barriers) and barriers within ourselves (internal barriers).

External Barriers to Motivation

External barriers include the nature of physical reality and the nature of other people. Physical reality imposes constraints. Gravity, scarcity, illness, and death all present barriers for us to address.

Then there are other people, who see their wants and needs as their priorities and which often, but not always, conflict with ours. They may have limited interest in our projects or limited skills to apply to them. They may be dishonest or incompetent, but they also often have complementary wants, needs, and motivations, which can be quite helpful.

External barriers present serious challenges, but they are external. By recognizing those barriers and applying knowledge, technology, skill, time, and effort, we can overcome many of them. In other words, we can work with the given resources and within the limitations of our world, social systems (such as the economy and the law), and other people—as long as we understand those resources and limitations and stay motivated.

Internal Barriers to Motivation

The barriers within us include things in our minds and bodies that undermine our ability to develop and maintain our motivation. I would like to be able to tell you that because these lay within us we have more control over them than we do over external barriers, but that's not necessarily true. Many carpenters have more control over the wood, tools, and skills they use than they do over their beliefs, thoughts, and behaviors.

Certain beliefs, thoughts, and behaviors can clearly hamper your motivation. Here are the items I see as the chief internal barriers to motivation:

Feeling undeserving: Many people undermine their motivation in at least some areas because they feel that they don't deserve to pursue, let alone achieve, their goals.

Fear: Fear takes many forms, including fear of success, failure, rejection, ridicule, and hard work.

Comparisons: It's natural to compare ourselves to others, but I can think of no better way to become hyperaware of your limitations.

Blame: The tendency to blame someone or something for a lack of motivation or accomplishment is among the most insidious internal enemies. That's because it so often seems to make sense. If you are trying to do something difficult, it can seem as if things are going against you. However, blame is among the least productive of all emotions. That's because it moves the feeling of control from within you to outside you.

When Does Life Begin?

Many people think their "real life" will begin at some point in the future. It may be when they graduate, marry, or reach a certain age. It may be a vaguer point, such as when they have enough money, move to a new city, or land a certain job. Other people go through life thinking that something will happen to transform them. Meanwhile, their lives are unfolding with minimal participation on their part.

Fantasy and Magical Thinking: Our imaginations can help or hinder our motivation. Imagination can be misapplied, and fantasy takes many forms. Some people believe they're creating salable music or art and that the music business and art galleries are conspiring against them.

Unlimited Possibilities: This is a form of fantasy in which you believe that you can do anything, but don't actually do much at all. Some people enjoy that feeling of potential, of possibilities, of a wonderful future so much that they never actually pursue an endeavor. In extreme cases, these folks avoid commitment to anything.

Unaddressed Underlying Problems: I'm generally skeptical of "medicalizing" certain personality problems. Yet, over the past twenty-five years, new diagnostic tools have enabled the psychiatric profession to more clearly diagnose many mental health problems. These problems often stem from brain chemistry imbalances, which can make life very tough for some people.

> Life is what happens when you are making other plans.
> —John Lennon (songwriter and musician)

Substance Abuse: This widespread problem truly undermines motivation. Many people who abuse alcohol and illegal and prescription drugs are self-medicating a mental health problem. Others are escaping feelings of inadequacy, low self-esteem, anger, frustration, or fatigue.

I realize there's a difference between use and abuse. A certain amount of use by way of "relaxing" is normal in our society, particularly in social situations. It's arguably even healthy to an extent for some people. Abuse is another story, for a few reasons:

○ *If you spend your days looking forward to happy hour, your focus is not on your goals and what's required to reach them.*

○ *Similarly, if you spend your evenings in a state of intoxication, that tends to*

Take Action
If you suspect that you have a substance abuse problem, and twelve step programs such as Alcoholics Anonymous don't appeal to you, check out SMART recovery programs at *www .smartrecovery.org*.

11

Are You Driven?

When someone says you have "a lot of drive," it's a compliment. It implies that you have energy, focus, and motivation. When we say someone is driven, however, negative implications arise. After all, automobiles and cattle are driven. There's a connotation of desperation and strain in "driven," as though the person's not really in charge. If you're driven to succeed, fine. But whenever possible, drive yourself.

become your motivation for getting through the day. In fact, getting through the day—rather than using the day—becomes the goal.

○ Finally, if you are hungover and fatigued from booze or drugs, you can't stay motivated to achieve what you want.

burn•out

1. loss of interest, focus, or energy regarding one or more parts of your professional or personal life

2. situation resulting from putting out effort without enough rest or rewards

If you even suspect that alcohol or drugs are affecting your motivation, or that you are abusing them, even at a "recreational" level, get counseling and modify your intake, or, better still, quit.

What About Kicking Back?

Does the image of the motivated individual repel you? Do you think that being motivated means thinking only about your goals and ways to reach them?

I hope not, because you don't have to become driven in order to be motivated. For most of us and for most goals, being motivated is not a matter of eating, drinking, sleeping, and breathing the same mission every hour of the day and night. (Of course, this leaves aside life-or-death situations, such as military combat and adventures in extreme conditions.)

In fact, sustaining motivation actually calls for taking time off from the pursuit of your goal, if for no other reason than to avoid burnout. Time away from a pursuit enables you to come back to it refreshed and with a new point of view. Rest is essential to productivity and to maintaining motivation, particularly for creative endeavors and for any long-term pursuit.

When's My Next Raise?

Early in my career, I eagerly anticipated and worked hard for raises and promotions. After each advance, I felt satisfied and proud for several weeks. But soon, those feelings faded and I started wondering about my next raise and promotion. Any new position soon became the new reality, with which I soon became dissatisfied. Ultimately, I focused more on job content than advancement, which led me to a writing career.

What Did He Say?

I attended a speakers' conference and, amid many useful sessions, found the featured speaker oddly useless. With the voice of a preacher and tears in his eyes, he told stories of people who walked again after horrible accidents, worked their way out of the ghetto, or founded great businesses in their kitchens. At the end, he told us we had the power to do these things too. It felt great, but we didn't receive any actual advice on how to accomplish any of our goals.

Endless Human Wants

People want things. Indeed, wanting things is part of human nature. As you will see, becoming motivated in useful ways means deciding what you want out of life and pursuing it. You cannot have everything. In fact, you cannot have everything you want. Given that, you may find yourself living a happier life if you want the things that you have as well as things that you don't have.

In fact, you can learn to want what you have—and to become motivated to keep it and appreciate it. This generally involves taking stock of what we have accomplished, appreciating the people we have in our lives, and understanding that although we are programmed to want things, we can decide what we really want and develop and direct our motivation into useful channels.

Motivation or Inspiration?

In this book I will, among other things, aim to describe systematic motivational methods rather than aim only to inspire you. I've heard a number of motivational speakers and have read quite a few books on motivation. But I've found most of the speakers and many of the books to be more inspirational than motivational.

I have nothing against inspiration. I love being inspired. But inspiration isn't the same as motivation. Inspiration is the feeling that you can and will do something. It's a feeling of empowerment and excitement, even when it is low key. Unfortunately, it is usually a fleeting feeling, and is shorter lived than motivation. It typically disappears when the source of inspiration disappears.

> I don't wait for moods. You accomplish nothing if you do that. Your mind must know it has got to get down to work.
> —**Pearl S. Buck (author)**

In other words, inspiration doesn't provide the commitment to a goal, a method for sustaining the feeling, or a program for changing from an unmotivated to a motivated state of mind. Remember, motivation is desire deep enough to move you to action.

The best motivational speakers and writers have programs for change or methods you can use to motivate yourself. Some of them include methods for acquiring the skills you need to accomplish the things you are trying to accomplish. They all recognize the difficulty of sustaining motivation, and of persevering when problems arise and setbacks occur, which is where discipline comes in.

Inspiration feels good and people like to feel good. We live in a feel-good society and much of what we do, we do in order to feel good. But motivation means working toward what you want even when you don't feel like it. It has to do with choosing long-term goals over short-term gratification.

A Matter of Maturity

I hate to sound judgmental, but I'll have to risk it: The ability to motivate yourself can be viewed as a matter of maturity. It requires that you decide what's important to you, what you want out of life, and what contribution you're prepared to make to this world. It also requires you to do something after you make those decisions.

Achieving maturity isn't easy. In adolescence, we try on various roles and identities. It's an awkward time when we try to figure out or decide who we are, what we're good at, what we enjoy, who we want to have as friends, who we want to be like, and how we will live in this world. Growing into adulthood means figuring those things out, or at least coming up with some provisional answers and then acting on them.

Many people extend their adolescence well into their twenties (and beyond). They may believe that they are trying to "find themselves" and maybe they are. But there's a good chance that some of us are so complex that the search could take a lifetime. Meanwhile, there are places to go, people to see, things to do.

In other words, to become motivated, decide to do something.

"

IF YOU PLAN ON BEING ANYTHING LESS
THAN **YOU ARE CAPABLE
OF BEING**, YOU WILL PROBABLY
BE UNHAPPY ALL THE DAYS OF YOUR
LIFE.

"

—Abraham Maslow
(psychologist)

Why Do We Do What We Do?

People have been wondering about what motivates people since ancient times. At the broadest level this is the study of human behavior: Why do people do what they do? The most scientific, systematic study of human behavior would be psychology. However, we're not going to look at all human behavior, just at motivation.

Psychologists and psychiatrists have spent considerable time studying motivation, and their studies have led to some interesting theories. Some of these theories provide practical guidance and answers to the question, "Why do we do what we do?" They help you understand what motivates people, including yourself.

So in this chapter we examine theories of motivation and what they have to do with us. When you know why you do what you do, you can better motivate yourself. When you know why other people do what they do, you can do a better job of motivating them.

About Motivational Theories

Notice that these theories focus on why people do what they do, rather than on what people *should* do. The should part is covered more by philosophy, which addresses questions about why we're alive, what constitutes "being," and the purpose of life. Religion looks at these issues from a spiritual perspective. As scientists, psychologists direct most of their energy toward explaining observable behavior.

In layman's terms, people do what they do because they want to; but that raises the question of why they want to do what they do. If you're considering lower-order needs—for example, needs dictated by the fact that you're alive, such as the need for water, food, and sleep—that's pretty straightforward. Thirst motivates you to drink; hunger motivates you to eat; and fatigue motivates you to sleep.

But even those basic needs can become complex. For example, some people are motivated to drink only bottled water, eat in pricey restaurants, and sleep on Egyptian cotton sheets. Why? In a way, they are connecting lower-order needs to higher-order needs, which have to do with the need for a sense of affiliation, status, and achievement. These more social needs motivate a tremendous amount of human behavior, so we'd best understand them as well.

> **so•cial needs**
>
> 1. need for recognition, public rewards, status, prestige, and a good reputation
>
> 2. needs that convert basic needs, such as clothing, housing, and cars, into status symbols

Not everyone is motivated by the same things, even when they are doing the exact same thing. For example, two boxers in a ring are each doing the same thing—fighting—with the same goal—to knock the other guy out. But one may be trying to show the world how physically powerful he is and the other may be in there only for the money. Please keep that in mind as we examine these motivational theories.

Two Major Types of Motivation

Most theories of motivation aim to identify, classify, and explain wants and needs. Some wants and needs are universal. For instance, everyone wants at least some social contact, and everyone needs to eat, drink, and sleep. However, some people are more motivated by some wants and needs than by others.

In general, there are two major types of motivation: internal motivation and external motivation. These are also known as intrinsic and extrinsic motivation. Intrinsic motivation lies within the person. The want or need springs from inside the person, whether it is hunger or thirst or a need to learn something or to control something. Extrinsic motivation lies outside the person. The want or need springs from something in the environment or something someone else does.

Each of us is subject to both internal and external motivators. One goal in becoming a motivated person is to understand various motivators as they affect you. Then, you can manage your motivation rather than be jerked around by your environment or

the•o•ry

1. set of principles or a model that explains the workings, causes, and effects of an event or behavior

2. hypothesis or unproven assumption about a phenomenon

other people. In and of themselves, internal and external motivations are neither good nor bad. The goal is to understand what is motivating you and why, and whether your response and the effects of your response to that motivator are good or bad for you.

The rest of this chapter covers major theories of motivation.

Maslow's Hierarchy of Needs

The hierarchy of needs developed by Abraham Maslow is probably the best-known classification of needs, and it's a great starting point for understanding motivation. Maslow categorized human needs into five groups:

- *Self-actualization needs*

- *Esteem needs*

- *Social needs*

- *Safety needs*

- *Physiological needs*

Maslow grouped needs according to their type and the order in which people seek to get them met. The hierarchy, starting with the lowest level needs, is as follows:

THEORISTS AND THEIR THEORIES

- Maslow's Hierarchy of Needs

- Alderfer's ERG Theory

- McClelland's Acquired Needs Theory

- Herzberg's Two-Factor Theory

- Skinner's Reinforcement Theory

- *At the bottom are physiological needs, the need for air, water, food, clothing, shelter, and sex.*

- *Then come safety needs, the need for physical and psychological safety, freedom from fear, and the need for an orderly environment.*

- *Next come social needs, the need for love and affection, for relationships and affiliation.*

- *Then come esteem needs, the need for respect from others, for attention, status, fame, and so on, and the need for a sense of self-respect, competence, and independence.*

- *Finally, at the top of the hierarchy is the need for what Maslow called self-actualization.*

The need for self-actualization is a bit fuzzier than the others. Maslow defined it mainly in terms of the kind of people he saw as "self-actualizers." He tried to define those people in terms of their characteristics. Essentially, the need for self-actualization finds expression as a need for a deep, inner sense of purpose and fulfillment in one's life.

Maslow believed that until the needs at each lower level were met, a person didn't focus on the needs at the next level. Some controversy surrounds this idea, but it is worth noting. After all, hungry people in war-torn countries don't worry about keeping up with the Joneses, which is rooted in social and esteem needs.

Take Action
Learn more about Maslow's ideas by reading Dr. C. George Boeree's synopsis of his life and work at *www.ship.edu/~cgboeree/maslow.html*.

The Nature of Needs

Maslow's classification of needs implies that some needs are physical, some are social, and some are almost metaphysical. By that I mean that the physical needs are met by tangible items and things you can see such as food, clothing, and sleep. Social needs are met by interactions with others. (Maslow classified sex as a physiological need, yet many people get along without it and it clearly relates to social and esteem needs.) Metaphysical needs are met when you feel that your accomplishments and your life meet certain internal or perhaps external (say, religious) standards that you have set for yourself or acquired.

Two implications of Maslow's theory are particularly important:

First, in affluent, market-driven, industrialized societies, people have transformed many basic needs into symbols of belongingness, achievement, and status. Many products are actually referred to by marketers and some consumers as "aspirational" products—products that people aspire to own.

> All the evidence that we have indicates that it is reasonable to assume in practically every human being ... there is an active will toward health, an impulse toward growth, or toward the actualization.
> —**Abraham Maslow (psychologist)**

This has made shopping something of a "self-actualizing" activity. This is spoofed in bumper stickers that say, "When the going gets tough, the tough go shopping," and, even more on the nose, "I shop, therefore I am." I see this as evidence of marketers deep knowledge of motivation, and—dare I say it?—a somewhat limited view of self-actualization on the part of some members of our society.

I suppose there's nothing wrong with actualizing yourself through acquisition of possessions, particularly if the alternative were crime. But in this book I maintain that it's good to be aware of what is motivating you. The fact that some people present themselves as ironically hyperaware of shopping being their way of actualizing themselves doesn't necessarily mean it's the best they can do.

Given the nefarious purposes people have devoted their lives to, there's nothing really wrong with believing that whoever has the most toys when he dies wins. Nor is there anything wrong with acting on that motivation, considering that it has moved many people to provide society with useful products and services. But I believe in choosing your motivation consciously. That way, you don't wind up realizing on your deathbed that you had another, non-shopping self that you might have spent your life actualizing.

Belongingness and Conformity

The second aspect of Maslow's hierarchy of needs that interests me is my suspicion that the need for belongingness and esteem may, for some of us, be linked to the feeling of undeservingness I mentioned in Chapter 1. The need for belongingness motivates us to socialize, make friends, join clubs, and participate in clubs and in our communities. The need for esteem—for the approval of others—motivates us to obtain degrees, dress well, and show up for work. Those are good things.

But the need for belongingness and others' approval can prompt behaviors that lead to mindless (or mindful) conformity. When the need to belong and to win others' approval prompts us to conform in ways that run contrary to our values and beliefs, then we might not be thinking for ourselves. If you're not thinking for yourself, you are not taking responsibility for your choices in life. You lose sight of what you want out of life. When you lose sight of what you want out of life, you stand little chance of getting it.

What Maslow's Hierarchy Means to Us

To me, the following three aspects of Maslow's hierarchy are the most relevant in understanding motivation:

First, in most industrialized nations, the "lower order" physiological and safety needs are met at a decent level for most of the population. This means that the higher order needs for esteem and self-actualization become more important. (Social needs include the need for family and other human contact, which is still fairly basic.)

Second, the need for esteem drives a lot of behavior in industrialized societies. We all want and need approval from others and ourselves, but it's useful to know which one is motivating you—your need for your own approval, or for the approval of others.

Third, for many people in affluent societies, esteem and self-actualization may be the key motivators much of the time. This is particularly true of the motivation that you need in order to achieve complex, long-term goals, such as completing your education, rearing children, or building a successful career.

Alderfer's ERG Theory

Clayton P. Alderfer refined or at least reclassified Maslow's categories of needs into those related to existence, relatedness, and growth—thus the designation of ERG Theory. In Alderfer's theory:

- *Existence needs are those that Maslow identified as physiological and safety needs.*

- *Relatedness needs are Maslow's social and esteem needs.*

- *Growth needs are Maslow's self-actualization needs.*

The Three Big Questions

It's been said that the three big questions are: Who am I? Who are the others? What are we doing here? ERG may parallel these questions. First, you are someone who needs certain things in order to exist. Second, you want to relate to other people. Third, we must all do something useful with our lives in order to grow and to actualize ourselves.

Aside from reclassifying the needs from five categories into three, the major contribution of ERG Theory is that Alderfer did not insist that the needs are a hierarchy, although he did believe that we had to feel physically comfortable (fed, rested, and so on) and safe before we pursued relationships.

McClelland's Acquired Needs Theory

David McClelland also theorized that three basic needs motivate us, although he didn't concern himself with Maslow's physiological or safety needs or Alderfer's existence needs. Instead, Alderfer felt that we were motivated by three acquired (or learned) needs, which were the needs for:

- *Achievement*

- *Affiliation*

- *Power*

McClelland theorized that each of us will tend to be motivated more by one of these three factors than by the other two:

- *People motivated by the need for achievement primarily want to accomplish things for the recognition it brings from others or for the internal satisfaction it brings, or both.*

- *People motivated by the need for affiliation primarily want to be with and relate to other people in close personal relationships or in groups, or both.*

- *People motivated by the need for power primarily want to control other people, either for personal or organizational goals.*

By leaving more basic physiological needs aside, McClelland's theory focuses more on psychological needs. Broadly, people motivated by achievement most want accomplishment; people motivated by affiliation most want relationships; and people motivated by power most want control over others.

Herzberg's Two-Factor Theory

Frederick Herzberg, who mainly studied motivation in the workplace, developed a two-factor theory in which he classified some needs as Hygiene factors and some as Motivators.

Hygiene factors are those things that must be present or people will become dissatisfied. They don't create satisfaction, but rather prevent dissatisfaction. In the workplace these generally include a comfortable environment, professional management, reasonable company policies, sociable coworkers, and good salary and benefits.

Motivators relate to higher-order needs (self-actualization needs) such as opportunities to grow professionally and personally, to work on breakthrough projects or products, or to express oneself or pursue socially useful or intellectually stimulating work.

Herzberg's concept of hygiene factors was quite important. Managers used to believe, for instance, that money was a far more powerful motivator than it actually is. They also underestimated how important good management was to workers. In other words, these two things are so basic that most workers, at least in industrialized nations, will be dissatisfied if they are absent.

Herzberg's concept of Motivators is also important, particularly when you are managing scientific or creative professionals. Many scientists and academics are motivated more by the content of their jobs—and the freedom to pursue the work that they find most intellectually challenging—than by money or the prestige of the institution.

B. F. Skinner's Reinforcement Theory

Most motivational theorists focus on needs, but some look more at the mechanisms that prompt people's actions. There's a difference between the two approaches, and Burrhus Frederic Skinner, an American psychologist, is the most well known of those focusing on mechanisms. B. F. Skinner is considered the founder of experimental psychology, also known as behaviorism. Skinner believed that animal and human behavior is shaped by learning and that learning occurs in response to conditions and events (stimuli) in the environment. That means that one can shape behavior, mainly others' behavior, by providing positive and negative reinforcement.

Skinner wanted to study behavior scientifically, which means recording observations, seeking

31

visible cause and effect, measuring phenomena, and experimenting to test and verify theories. Many of Skinner's experiments, which he called operant conditioning, were performed on laboratory rats that were given food pellets for certain behaviors and mild electric shocks for others.

Skinner's Key Ideas

Here are the key ideas from Skinner's work:

op•er•ant con•di•tion •ing

1. method of shaping behavior with positive and negative reinforcement

2. system in which reinforcement and behavior are measurable

3. common methods of training dogs are essentially operant conditioning

○ *Positive reinforcement strengthens a behavior by rewarding the subject—that is, the person or animal—when he performs it. For instance, if someone gives you a ten dollar bill for every day you go without smoking, you're getting positive reinforcement.*

○ *Negative reinforcement, which differs from punishment, strengthens a behavior by removing, or enabling the subject to end or avoid something bad. If you stop smoking for a day and you cough less, you're getting negative reinforcement.*

- Punishment weakens a behavior by providing a bad consequence for the subject when he engages in the behavior. If someone raps your knuckles with a ruler every time you reach for a cigarette, you're being punished.

- Extinction weakens a behavior by providing no rewards for it. If you quit smoking and receive or perceive no benefit, you may go back to it.

Skinner also believed that the schedule of reinforcement would affect the learning or unlearning of behavior:

- Continuous reinforcement provides the reinforcement every time the behavior is performed.

- Intermittent reinforcement provides the reinforcement some of the time that the behavior is performed, rather than every time.

Implications of Skinner's Work

For anyone interested in motivation, Skinner's ideas have implications, including the following:

- Positive reinforcement generally works better than other methods when it comes to strengthening a behavior. As they say, "You'll catch more flies with honey than with vinegar."

- *Punishment generally tends to be less effective than other methods because people focus on avoiding the punishment rather than extinguishing the behavior. Patterns of criminal behavior tend to bear this out.*

- *If you reward a behavior, then stop rewarding it, you may extinguish it. People may become demotivated when they perceive something positive being removed, unless they see other rewards for performing the behavior.*

Teacher Learns from Students

In a perhaps apocryphal case, students in a college psychology course shaped their professor's behavior during lectures. They would look down, fidget, and ignore him when he lectured from one side of the room, and pay close attention to him when lectured from the other side. Over time, they managed to reinforce his behavior so that he stood mainly on the side where they gave him the positive reinforcement.

- *Similarly, continuous reinforcement often leads people to believe that they should always be rewarded for the behavior. This occurs in companies in which people receive a bonus several years in a row, and come to see it as part of their compensation rather than a reward for extra effort. When people expect the bonus, they won't work harder for it.*

> **KEEP DOING** WHAT YOU'VE BEEN DOING AND YOU WILL **KEEP GETTING** WHAT YOU'VE BEEN GETTING.

—Jackie B. Cooper
(automotive sales
training executive)

3

How Motivational Methods Work

Having examined the scientific side of motivation in the previous chapter, in this chapter we turn to an overview of how motivational methods work in general. Most of what I'm discussing here refers to popular motivational methods, literature, and experts.

Various motivational methods work in various ways. Some rely heavily on rational thinking, decision making, and willpower. Others work more with the imagination, the subconscious, and the spiritual side of a person. I believe that the best methods tap both our rational thinking processes and our imaginations. This chapter provides an overview of how the various methods work so you can see the mechanisms they rely on and be positioned to decide which specific methods—which I cover in Chapter 4—appeal most to you.

Popular Motivational Methods

When I refer to methods of motivation as "popular"—such as positive thinking, visualization, and hypnosis—I am not putting them down. I and millions of other people have used them to motivate ourselves. Rather, I mean that they have usually not been validated through scientific studies. These methods rest more on common sense and practical application—on "what works for you"—than on rigorous theory and experimentation. Indeed, their effectiveness can depend on blind faith and your ability to talk yourself into a given state of mind or course of action. But if the method motivated you to do what you needed to do, then it worked.

> **vi•su•al•i•za•tion**
>
> 1. mental images of our performance, feelings, or results in a situation or effort
>
> 2. potentially powerful motivational tool, especially for envisioning actions and outcomes

The issue and industry of self-motivation, self-improvement, and self-management has spawned many ideas that have demonstrated practical value—and acquired legions of fans—without scientific experimentation or validation. A book that surveys motivation would be incomplete if it omitted these methods. And when you consider that they tend to use commonsense approaches and well-known concepts, such as willpower and decision making, most of them do have an internal logic that I'll explain in this chapter.

Will, Imagination, and Purpose

When you examine popular methods of self-motivation from the "soft" standpoint as opposed to the "scientific" standpoint, three basic elements emerge:

- *Purpose and goals*
- *Willpower*
- *Imagination*

Purpose and Goals

Virtually every method of motivation assumes that you have a purpose to fulfill or a goal that you want to achieve—or requires you to develop one. A purpose or goal serves as the focus of your motivation. You need motivation to achieve a purpose or goal, usually because the purpose or goal is difficult, complex, or long-term. Purposes and goals are two different, but related, things, as I explain below.

Purpose Is a High-Level Concept

In motivational methods, the purpose refers to one or both of two things:

First, your purpose can be the overall mission you are trying to accomplish, something outside yourself that you want to make a reality. For instance, your purpose in becoming a law enforcement officer may be to make the world safer or your purpose in making a film may be to tell the truth about the perfume industry. You then can use that purpose to motivate yourself to do the things you must do to become a law enforcement officer or to make that film.

Second, your purpose can be your self-concept or your ideas about your destiny or life's meaning. Most philosophical systems and all religions focus on purpose in this way. Purpose in this sense relates to your values and your ideas about life's meaning. For example, you might say that the purpose of life, or perhaps the highest purpose in life, is to relieve human suffering (Mother Teresa), to enjoy all the pleasures this world has to offer (Hugh Hefner), or to express oneself (Madonna).

Again, I am not here to tell you your purpose. I am only pointing out that many methods of motivation call for you to consider your purpose.

Goals Are More Concrete

A goal is something you can define clearly, something you can accomplish and know when you've accomplished it. It's also something you can accomplish by performing certain tasks, usually in a certain order.

In general, goals are more tangible and concrete than purposes. You may set out to make the world a safer place or to expose the truth about the perfume industry and find that there's no way to know whether or not you have succeeded. The world may remain as violent as ever, and the perfume industry, like most industries, does both good and bad. But you will know whether or not you became a police officer or made the movie, because those are concrete goals.

Take Action
If you wonder about the meaning of life, read *Man's Search for Meaning* by Viktor E. Frankl, one of the best books ever published on the subject.

Virtually all motivational methods advise you to set goals. In fact, many methods state that you should (a) have a higher purpose and (b) set goals that will help you fulfill that purpose. In other words, if you want the world to be a safer place, you can become a police officer, or you could become a prosecutor in the district attorney's office, a teacher, or any number of other things. Your goals should serve your purpose.

Willpower

Some people equate willpower with motivation. They feel that "if you really want to do something you will do it." There's some truth to that, but only some. For one thing, as noted in Chapter 1, each of us has conflicting wants. So motivation often becomes an issue of which thing you want more. Motivation often comes down to getting yourself to do the thing that you want to do less at a given moment in order to get something you want more at a later time.

The act of doing the thing you want more in the long term rather than what you want in the short term is called delaying gratification. We will discuss delayed gratification in some depth, because it's key in motivation. I find it useful to think of willpower as the ability to delay gratification. You do the thing

de·layed grat·i·fi·ca·tion

1. acting upon a longer-term goal rather than a conflicting short-term want

2. controlling impulsive behavior that can undermine your goals

you know you "should" do given your long-term goals, rather than what you want to do for immediate gratification.

I believe it's a mistake to equate motivation with willpower. I find it more useful to view willpower, and the ability to delay gratification, as components of motivation. It's part of what you need, a skill you need, to maintain your motivation. You need willpower to decide what you want to do—that is, to commit to a goal—and then to help you maintain your commitment when competing desires or setbacks occur.

But willpower is not the whole story, and most motivational experts agree. That's why they stress the role of the imagination.

Where Did You Grow Up?

Motivation varies across cultures and generations. Some cultures value conformity, and if you're not motivated to conform you may be seen as uninterested in success. This tends to be so in Japan, and among Americans in the World War II generation. Others, such as current U.S. culture, emphasize self-interest and self-expression. Culture affects the values and behaviors that are rewarded and reinforced and thus affects motivation.

Imagination Is Funny

Most of the motivational methods aim to help you harness the imagination as a motivational tool. Skeptics and those wedded to the so-called Protestant work ethic may see this as a way of avoiding the need for willpower or as magical thinking, and sometimes it is. However, I believe our imaginations represent a real motivational resource.

Here are four ways in which the imagination works in motivational systems:

> Because gratification of a desire leads to the temporary stilling of the mind and the experience of the peaceful, joyful Self it's no wonder that we get hooked on thinking that happiness comes from the satisfaction of desires.
> **—Joan Borysenko (psychologist and medical scientist)**

- *Your imagination fuels your emotions in ways that rational thinking and willpower cannot. Motivation is a feeling, so these methods help you use your imagination to affect your feelings in positive ways.*

- *It's easy to imagine the worst unless you use your imagination in positive ways. You can imagine that barriers are insurmountable, that you can never develop the skills needed to reach your goals, and that you will surely fail, and these are not helpful images. Or you can imagine the opposite. Motivational methods show you* how to use your imagination to produce helpful images.

○ Your imagination helps you deal with subconscious issues that you can't always address with willpower. By definition, a subconscious issue is one you're not aware of, so your imagination, which works more from the subconscious than the conscious mind, can be a power- ful tool for dealing with subconscious enemies of motivation, such as fear of success or fear of failure.

○ Your imagination can help you leap over logical barriers to success. For instance, it was quite logical for people to believe you couldn't land a man on the moon. People cannot breath in outer space. Bringing the astronaut back presented huge difficulties. But people could imagine landing a man on the moon and that image motivated them to develop the technologies and processes for accomplishing the goal.

IMAGINATION HELPS MOTI- VATION BY

○ Generating emotions

○ Producing inspiring images

○ Addressing subconscious barriers

○ Blasting away logical barriers

A Bit More on Imagination

Many motivational methods stress the role of visualization,

mental images, and seeing
yourself in a certain way. I
have nothing against these
methods and have found
that they can work for me
and for other people. Some
people, however, find it dif-
ficult to produce or sustain
mental images. Their brains
are just not wired that way.
Other people judge the idea
of using their imaginations

in these ways to be hokey or see it as a "New Age"
technique and they dislike anything of that nature.

If you have difficulty engaging in visualization or
producing mental images or you don't feel comfort-
able using them or judge them to be useless, that's
okay. But I would suggest that you give these meth-
ods a good try before dismissing them. If they don't
work for you, please know that working with the
imagination goes beyond visualization and mental
imagery.

Words of Caution

If you are looking for ways to motivate yourself, it's
easy to jump around among various methods or
"gurus." As you read this book and others on motiva-
tion, examine your responses to various methods. If
something makes sense, investigate it more deeply
and try a few of the tools and techniques.

Some of these methods are compilations of common sense. For instance, the idea of "thinking positively" will make sense to most of us. On the other hand, what must you do to think positively? Do you have to banish every "negative thought" from your mind, as if that's possible here on planet Earth? Or is it okay to think positively most of the time, or about your area of endeavor, or about yourself and other people?

My approach has always been to mix and match methods, tools, and techniques to fit my situation, goals, state of mind, needs, and skills or lack thereof.

There can be a chicken-and-egg element in certain efforts to motivate yourself. For instance, to use most motivational methods you must be motivated to use them. Well, if you are motivated to use a motivational method, why do you need a motivational method? Also, if you use the motivational method and it doesn't work, does that mean you weren't motivated enough? Or does it mean that you didn't use it correctly or applied it to the "wrong" goals?

There can also be an insidious side to certain concepts in motivation. Take the idea that your thinking determines the quality of your life, a common concept in popular motivational literature. Several negative outcomes can emerge from this idea, including notions that:

> ○ *You are "failing" if you cannot control*
> *your thinking in ways that motivate*

you. This adds a layer of demotivating thoughts to whatever you are already wrestling with. In other words, you can start feeling bad not only about being unmotivated, but also about failing to get the motivational method to work.

○ *You are repelling other people with your thoughts. If indeed you are repelling people, it's far more likely that certain behaviors of yours may be less than engaging.*

○ *You can attract money to you just by thinking about money. Yes, you can develop an attitude of prosperity, but you must also do things that will make you money.*

○ *Your thoughts are making you ill. Some people believe that their thoughts can produce illness—even cancer or heart disease. Although there may be a "mind-body connection," the major determiners of health are lifestyle, genes, and so on.*

Clearly, some thought patterns are better than others. Only an idiot would argue that your thinking has nothing to do with the quality of your life. But that doesn't necessarily imply that it's the only thing that matters or even that it matters more than anything else. Indeed, your actions matter more than anything. To the extent that thinking determines behavior—and, to a great extent, it does—thinking is important to your success. Yet that doesn't mean that you must try to control your thinking or that if you do control it then you can control anything, other than your behavior.

Is This About Kidding Yourself?

It would be easy for some people to think that motivating yourself, particularly with some of the methods in the next chapter, is a way of kidding yourself. In a sense it may be, but if it works I see no problem. Call it managing your motivation, manipulating yourself, or playing mind games. Whatever you call it, if it's not harmful, then it may be useful.

For instance, one of the first proponents of positive affirmations, also known as autosuggestion, was Émile Coué. Coué was a French psychologist and pharmacist, famous for the phrase, "Every day, in every way, I am getting better and better." He asked his patients and, in his book *Self-mastery through Conscious Auto-suggestion*, his readers to repeat this phrase to themselves. This book was published in England in 1920 and in the United States in 1922.

Some people find the idea laughable, particularly the idea of repeating the statement to yourself in the mirror every morning, which some practitioners recommend. Yet other people have had success with it. This method resembles other forms of autosuggestion, notably hypnosis, and ways of "programming" the subconscious in positive ways.

Let's face it: There are various levels of self-deception in this world. If you "program your mind" so you become more confident in job interviews or when dealing with sales prospects, you won't do much damage and may become more relaxed and effective. The danger would be programming your mind so you believe you have money coming in that is not coming in or you are free of a medical diagnosis that you actually have. That's carrying things way too far.

Motivation, Morality, and "The Universe"

I am not going to make moral judgments in this book, or at least I will keep them to an absolute minimum and flag any that I consciously make. I personally believe in living and letting live, and in exerting your rights to the extent you wish without violating the rights of others. So I am not going to pass judgment on what you are motivated to do. I would, however, hope that you would aim to achieve something that does you and someone else, and perhaps some larger population, some good.

In a way, motivation is neutral. If you want to fight against injustice or care for the least fortunate in this world, you're going to need motivation. If you are going to become a world class gambler or a junk food distributor, you need motivation. But I say *in a way* for a reason. Many people, myself included, believe that motivation that's tied to some higher and useful purpose, even if it only involves achieving your (safe, legal, useful) destiny or making your (safe, legal, useful) dream come true, will be the most powerful and sustainable form of motivation.

Some people, including some of the motivational "gurus" you'll meet in this book, believe that when you are motivated by your deepest need to express yourself, to redress a wrong, or to make something right in your life or in this world, you will actually find support from people and in ways that would not otherwise occur. This phenomenon has a few different names, but the most common and descriptive is synchronicity. It refers to the belief that the world or, if you prefer, the universe—or at least people and events—will support you when you are truly and deeply committed to making something good happen in your life and in this world.

I believe that too, because I've seen it time and again in my own life and in the lives of others I've known and read about.

syn•chro•nic•i•ty

1. situations in which supportive or meaningful events happen inexplicably

2. word coined by psychologist Carl Jung to describe meaningful patterns of events that cannot be explained

3. phenomenon summed up as "There are no accidents"

MOTIVATION IS A **FIRE FROM WITHIN**.

—Stephen Covey
(author)

4 Popular Methods of Motivation

Various methods of motivation have been developed, taught, and popularized by people who are in the motivation business. These folks mainly include motivational authors and speakers, although some of them are theorists and thinkers working more in the areas of self-improvement and personal growth. In this chapter, I'm going to summarize the ideas of several of these practitioners, so you have a general idea of what's out there in the way of motivational methods. I'll also discuss one or two methods that are not associated with any single expert.

I am mainly going to discuss the methods I have used and my experience with them. Therefore, this information has a subjective quality to it. I've chosen methods that appeal to me and that have somehow helped me develop or maintain my motivation. So, two caveats are in order: First, I haven't tried every method that's out there; and second, your experiences and results may differ from mine.

Two "Classic" Methods

Two of the oldest methods of self-motivation are positive thinking and its cousin, prosperity thinking. I say they are cousins because both methods rest on the notion that what you think will affect your attitude, behavior, and results. These methods hold that "good thoughts" lead to a motivated attitude, useful behavior, and positive results. These methods also hold that "bad thoughts" lead to lack of motivation, aimless or harmful behavior, and negative results.

Those premises are hard to refute, but in my opinion the methods have been surpassed by newer, more sophisticated approaches. That said, a positive frame of mind certainly can't hurt, and thinking does affect your attitude, behavior, and even results.

TOP MOTIVATIONAL PROFESSIONALS

- Tony Robbins
- Brian Tracy
- Dennis Waitley
- Wayne Dyer
- Zig Ziglar

Positive Thinking

Positive thinking means exactly that: You think positive thoughts and avoid negative ones. You think positive thoughts about yourself and your goals, your plans, and your ability to act. You think positive thoughts about the people in your life and the people you meet. If possible, you think positive thoughts about the world and the situations that it presents to you.

Norman Vincent Peale can be safely viewed as the first popular proponent of positive thinking, at least as a formal motivational tool. This is largely due to his best-selling book, *The Power of Positive Thinking*, which was published in 1952 and has sold over 20 million copies worldwide.

> Action springs not from thought, but from a readiness for responsibility.
> —**Dietrich Bonhoeffer (German theologian)**

In his landmark book, Dr. Peale presented ideas and techniques for overcoming self-doubt and worry. The book is somewhat dated, but it presents inspiring anecdotes and ideas, many of which are rooted in Christianity, given that Dr. Peale was a minister.

Positive thinking will help you address or avoid many of the enemies of motivation covered in Chapter 1. For instance, with positive thinking, you can banish or bypass enemies of motivation such as blame, comparisons, and fear of failure or success. Unfortunately, positive thinking itself won't bring results, nor will it necessarily even get you to act—and the key issue

The Power of Negative Thinking

Personally, I have found negative thinking—of a certain type—to be motivating. Fear of looking bad motivates me to prepare for presentations so that I'll be certain to look good. I found the nagging sense that I was wasting my life working for other people in a boring setting quite motivating. Negative thinking about employers (and some of my bosses) motivated me to become a self-employed writer.

in motivation is taking action. You have to think positively and act positively.

As a motivational approach, positive thinking has its pluses and minuses. On the upside, you can cultivate a positive, can-do attitude and that attitude will probably motivate you more than a negative, can't-do attitude. Also, most (but not all) people enjoy being around positive people. On the downside, you may try to control your thoughts to an extreme degree or feel bad about your thoughts, which can be difficult to distinguish from your feelings, which are even harder to control. Also, some people can't stand to be around those who have an unflaggingly positive attitude.

Earl Nightingale, Positive Thinker

Another pioneer in the motivational field was Earl Nightingale, an extremely accomplished salesman and an entrepreneur, who was a cofounder of Nightingale-Conant, one of the world's largest companies in the business of publishing and distributing motivational books, tapes, and courses. His inspirational recording The Strangest Secret, which grew out of pep talks he used to give the salespeople in his insurance agency, was the first spoken word recording to sell more than a million copies.

> You become what you think about.
> —Earl Nightingale (entrepreneur and author)

Prosperity Thinking

For my money, prosperity thinking is one of the more offbeat motivational methods. Although prosperity thinking is widely considered a New Age method, the seminal text on the subject is the classic book *Think and Grow Rich* by Napoleon Hill first published in 1937. I found the book inspiring but a bit repetitive given that the core message is in the title. I also found some of the techniques, such as forging the "Mastermind Alliance," somewhat elusive. Yet, millions of readers love this book and find it motivating.

Take Action
For a tremendous selection of inspirational and motivational books, tapes, and programs, check out *www.nightingale.com*, the Web site of Nightingale-Conant, the largest U.S. company in the business.

The core of prosperity thinking, also known as "prosperity consciousness" and "thinking abundantly," and sometimes mocked as "meditating for a Mercedes," is that if you think about money in positive ways, money will come to you. It's shot through with ideas like "money is energy" and the "laws of attraction." The notion is that some people repel money with negative thoughts about it and others attract it with their thinking.

There's a clear and sensible rationale to prosperity thinking, which is that if you think about money in positive ways, you will be more likely to engage in behaviors that make money and bring it to you. I and a number of people I know have gone through periods when we didn't seem terribly interested in money. We were slow to send out invoices and didn't pay attention to our investments. Guess what? Our collections slowed down and our investments earned less than they could have.

Like positive thinking, prosperity thinking has its positives and negatives. On the plus side, it can help you develop a healthier, more positive attitude toward money, if you need one. On the minus side, it can lead to a form of magical thinking in which you believe your thoughts themselves can attract money. You "attract" money when you take action to make money.

Rational Motivational Methods

Positive thinking and prosperity thinking mainly aim to harness the imagination. In contrast, rational motivational methods direct you to think logically about what you want and what you must do to obtain or achieve what you want. The best of these methods, which I'll discuss in this section, guide you to formulate goals you can commit to, to define what you must do to reach those goals, and to Take Action that moves you toward your goals.

The best of these methods also recognize that feelings such as blame, fear of rejection, and fear of success or failure undermine motivation. These methods suggest ways of dealing rationally with those feelings. For example, they recommend that you rationally examine your

mag•i•cal think•ing

1. belief that thinking something will happen will somehow make it happen

2. form of denial based on the idea that not thinking about problems makes them go away

fears. You say to yourself, "What is there really to fear? I'm not a soldier on a battlefield. I'm a business person on a sales call. Part of the process is hearing people say 'No' as I move toward 'Yes,'" and so on.

These methods often suggest that you write about the emotions that undermine your motivation, and I have found that to be quite valuable. They also often suggest that you make two columns and list the good and the bad things you're deriving from your current inaction, and the good and bad things you would derive from taking action.

The drawback with rational motivational methods is that they tend to assume that people will, when given a rational choice, choose rationally. In a way, they rely almost solely on willpower to resolve conflicting wants and situations of immediate versus long-term gratification. In sum, they assume that you have a good amount of discipline. That's fine, as long as you're aware that emotions often undermine discipline and that you may have to address those emotions with methods other than rational decision making— that is, with methods like hypnosis that operate more at an emotional level. My favorite rational approaches come from the psychologist Albert Ellis, who developed Rational Emotive Behavior Therapy (REBT).

The Rational Emotive Behavior Method

Albert Ellis developed an approach to his patients and in his books that he calls Rational Emotive Behavioral Therapy. It relies far more heavily on the rational than the emotive. Dr. Ellis presents his approach in his books *How to Refuse to Make Yourself Miserable about Anything, Yes Anything* and *A Guide to Rational Living.*

Essentially, Dr. Ellis sums up his approach as A-B-C, in which A equals Adversities or Adversaries, B equals our Beliefs about the adversities, and C equals the Consequences of various courses of action. For example, if you aim to become a successful actor, writer, or salesperson, you must cope with rejection. So let's let A equal rejection, B equal our beliefs about rejection, and C equal the consequences of various responses to rejection.

If you encounter rejection (A) and believe (B) that it means you have no acting, writing, or selling talent, you may decide to quit the field after experiencing rejection and as a consequence (C) give up before you really begin. If instead you encounter rejection (A) and you believe (B) that means you must improve your acting, writing, or selling skills, then you will work on those skills and consequently (C) either improve to the point where you see some success or not. If you see success, you will know that you've improved and are on the right path. If you don't see success, then you can decide that you have no acting, writing, or selling talent or that you need to improve even further.

Conversations with Yourself

Ellis basically recommends having logical conversations with yourself about what you think about reality, about actual reality, and about what you can—and cannot—do about reality. It's almost a

Zen way of thinking that says, if something bothers you, change it or avoid it; if you can't change it or avoid it, then don't let it bother you. This resembles the Serenity Prayer: "Lord give me the serenity to accept the things that I cannot change, the courage to change the things that I can change, and the wisdom to know the difference."

> If something is irrational, that means it won't work. It's usually unrealistic. . . . Rational beliefs bring us closer to getting good results in the real world.
> —**Albert Ellis**
> **(psychologist)**

The logical, thinking-through process that Dr. Ellis recommends is key to using REBT as a motivational approach. It leads you to see reality and to decide how you are going to deal with it. For example, suppose you are a salesperson and you are not making enough sales to earn a good living because you are not prospecting enough because you hate rejection.

You might analyze this situation along the following lines:

- *Is the rejection causing me actual physical, mental, emotional, or financial and professional harm? (Assess the harm that rejection—and avoiding rejection—is doing.)*

- *How is rejection—and avoiding rejection—helping me? (List the things that rejection is helping you do, such as eliminating people who won't buy, and things that avoiding it is doing, such as saving your feelings.)*

o *Are there ways that I can reduce or avoid rejection in sales? (Here you consider ways to reduce the rejection, such as finding better prospects. You can even consider quitting the sales profession.)*

o *Which of these things am I willing to do to reduce or avoid rejection? (If you're not willing to quit sales and you cannot eliminate all rejection, then you have to accept some.)*

o *What's more important to me: to avoid rejection or to remain in sales? (You must accept the fact that a certain amount of rejection comes with the sales territory.)*

o *How can I deal with the rejection most effectively? How can I use rejection to become a better salesperson? (You must devise strategies for dealing with rejection and for lessening its emotional effect.)*

Again, rational methods of motivation assume that you can conduct this kind of analysis rationally. The key with such methods is to be very honest with yourself. For example, if you hate rejection so much that it ruins your workdays and, even after this analysis, you make fewer sales calls, then perhaps you're not cut out for sales. Even after rational analysis, your feelings about rejection may trump your rational thoughts about it. If so, you must use other methods to deal with your feelings about rejection or admit that your feelings are strong enough to prompt a preference for another line of work.

Just Imagine

I've had real success with motivation methods that harness the imagination, particularly when I've used them to pursue specific goals. The two methods I've had the most success with are hypnosis and a version of neural linguistic programming.

Hypnosis

If you are unfamiliar with hypnosis, or familiar with it mainly through movies and television, please read this section with an open mind.

Hypnosis is a state of deep physical and mental relaxation which provides more ready access to the subconscious than a waking or sleeping state does. Most people describe this state as a trance, "zoning out," or something between sleep and wakefulness. It's not meditation because you're not trying to empty your mind or let thoughts pass through it. Yet it resembles meditation because you're in a relaxed but conscious state of mind. This state of mind leaves you open to post-hypnotic suggestion.

Here's what this has to do with motivation. If, indeed, some barriers to motivation are subconscious, then hypnosis may help you eliminate or work around those barriers. In fact, even if the barriers are conscious—for example, a conscious belief that you cannot learn to swim—hypnosis may help you change that belief.

post·hyp·not·ic sug·ges·tion

1. belief or behavior suggested to a person in a state of hypnosis

2. phrase stated to effect change in a person under hypnosis

Misconceptions About Hypnosis

Because hypnosis represents a mildly altered state of consciousness, some people feel funny about it. Depictions in movies and on TV of people barking like dogs, taking off their clothes, or committing crimes under hypnosis haven't helped matters.

Here are misconceptions about hypnosis, and the corresponding truth:

Hypnosis Myths

People can hypnotize you against your will. They cannot; in fact, the physician who helped me to quit smoking with hypnosis insisted that all hypnosis is self-hypnosis, and I've found that to be true for myself.

People will do crazy things under hypnosis. Actually, people won't do anything under hypnosis that is against their will. Stage hypnotists skillfully choose subjects who will be willing to act in an uninhibited manner on stage once they are under hypnosis.

People under hypnosis are in a zombie-like state of mind. As noted, it's really a state of deep physical and mental relaxation.

Hypnotists are oddballs who have you look at a dangling pocket watch and exert their will over you. Most hypnotists are psychiatrists, psychologists, or other mental health professionals working with clients. The watch is rarely used today, although hypnotists do use gentle, monotonic speech patterns and suggest that subjects imagine a relaxing environment, such as a pasture or a beach.

Neuro-Linguistic Programming

Neuro-linguistic programming (NLP) is a method for "programming" the mind with beliefs and behaviors that you see as desirable. NLP holds that because we think in language and images, we can program our minds with language and images. It also rests on the idea that if you don't program your mind, someone else will—advertisers, newscasters, teachers, and so on.

Some people see NLP as nonsense while others swear by it. I use the parts that work for me, and I don't worry about the rest. That's because I want practical methods whether or not there is science behind them. I might prefer science, but studies on NLP tend to be inconclusive.

Again, most methods work because people say they work, and a lot of people say they've been helped by NLP, especially as developed and presented by Anthony Robbins.

Anthony Robbins and NLP

People have mixed feelings regarding Tony Robbins, but I find his ideas and methods interesting and useful in many ways. I personally don't like events in which people get pumped up by evangelist-style leaders who tightly control the proceedings (down to the bathroom breaks) and use what I consider overly dramatic methods (like fire-walking) to make their point. Tony Robbins holds those types of events, which I have not attended. But many people do enjoy and benefit from those events and I have not read of anyone being harmed at them, beyond a few cases of burned feet.

What I like are Robbins's ideas about beliefs and how beliefs relate to behaviors. Robbins has written that our beliefs determine our actions, and that we can choose and change our beliefs. This makes sense to me. If you stop and think about it, there are empowering beliefs, such as, "I can quit smoking when I want to," and disempowering beliefs, such as "I'll never be able to quit smoking." Robbins shows how to change your beliefs to more empowering ones, or at least how to start thinking in more empowering ways.

Take Action

For a full primer on Anthony Robbins's methods, check out *Unlimited Power* (Free Press, reprint edition, 1997) and *Awaken the Giant Within* (Free Press, reprint edition, 1992).

Tony Robbins has what he calls a powerful "technology for change." His books describe, in great detail, how he believes our minds work and how you can manage your mind so you become more motivated, goal oriented, and able to take action to achieve your goals.

There are, of course, obvious limits to this technology for change, which is an extension of NLP and which Tony Robbins calls neuroassociative conditioning. For instance, while it may theoretically be possible for anyone to, say, mimic the mental state and physical movements of Eric Clapton, I have strong doubts that doing so could enable anyone to play the guitar like he does. However, despite such limitations, Robbins has many useful things to say about motivation and achieving goals.

But Wait, There's More

This overview of motivational methods only scratches the surface of what's out there. My main goal in this chapter is to give you a taste of how these methods work and what they rely on—rational thinking, imagination, or some combination of the two—and to tell you what has worked for me.

PRACTICAL MOTIVATION

part

2

"
THE QUESTION IS NOT WHETHER WE
WILL DIE, BUT **HOW WE WILL
LIVE**.
"

—Joan Borysenko
(psychologist and
medical scientist)

5

What's It All About? Purpose

In order to become and stay motivated, you must be doing something that you believe is worth doing, and pursuing something that you believe is worth pursuing. The things that you do and pursue are entirely up to you. That is the first thing many people have to learn about motivation—that our decisions about our purpose and goals and about how we spend our time and lives are up to us.

Many things conspire against us when we try to discover our purpose, choose our goals, and decide what to do with our time and our lives. In this chapter, we examine those things and how to deal with them. In the process, you can learn to discover or decide what you really want to be doing.

The Object of Your Motivation

On one level, becoming motivated is simply an issue of having the right purpose (one you believe is important) and choosing the right goals (those that you want to achieve given your purpose). As noted in Chapter 2, we all have wants and needs that we're motivated to fulfill. To understand motivation, let's for a moment consider a hypothetical, but very clear, want and need. Let's consider a situation in which what you want and need is so clear that you don't even have to think about motivation.

Suppose you were in a burning building. It's not your home, and you are the only one there. You smell smoke, you hear crackling, and now you see flames. What do you want and need? What do you do? You want and need to get out of that building, and that's what you do. You are motivated to flee. You don't think about it. You don't rationalize it. You don't harness your imagination. You don't need to "get motivated." You only need to get moving.

When you really want to do something, you do it. You may encounter difficulties and setbacks. You may succeed or fail. But you won't sit around wondering about whether or not to do it. You won't think about where you'll get the motivation, because you'll be too busy doing what you're motivated to do.

That's motivation—motivation so intense that you don't even think about it. That's what I want you to develop.

How do you develop that kind of motivation?

Make Up Your Mind

To develop deep motivation you have to make up your mind. That's a funny phrase, when you think about it.

Generally, "make up your mind" means to decide something, usually after mulling it over. But to "make up" something is also to fabricate it, in the way you "make up" a story or "make up" an excuse. In a way, many of us would do well to make up our minds in that sense.

After all, we all hold an internal dialogue (or is it a monologue?) with ourselves, in which we are the hero, victim, artist, audience, director, actor, performer, viewer, judge, jury, perpetrator, and arresting officer. But for what purpose? Most of us let our lives happen. People who accomplish things in this world are those who either discover or decide what their purpose is, choose goals that support that purpose, and then define the activities that move them toward those goals. In other words, they make up their minds about what they want to do.

You've had the experience of being motivated, even if you haven't been in any burning buildings lately. For instance, you've probably gone to a restaurant recently, looked at the menu and decided what you wanted to eat. Before that, you decided which restaurant to go to. Before that, you decided what kind of food you wanted and in what atmosphere and price range. Before that, you decided you were hungry, or that you wanted to have lunch or dinner with someone. These were everyday decisions, no big deal.

THE THREE KEY ELEMENTS

- Purpose
- Goals
- Tasks

You may say, "Yes, but deciding what you want to do with your life, and which goals to pursue, are a bigger deal. If we order the wrong dish, we've blown one meal and maybe $25. If we choose the wrong career, profession, city, or spouse, we might ruin a good chunk of our lives."

That, right there, is one of the problems people have when trying to decide what they really want: They think it's a life-or-death decision and then choose not to make it!

If it's such an important decision, don't you think it's important enough to make? You would think so, but several things work against making big decisions like these. So, we're going to look at what works against our making these decisions, and what to do about it.

You Get to Decide

If you were to learn only one thing from this book, I would want it to be this: You get to decide what to do with your life. It is an awesome responsibility, which is why so many people avoid it. The tragedy is that they effectively let someone else make the decision for them. They let someone else dictate their lives, goals, and pastimes.

So first, at a very fundamental level, you need to be motivated to take responsibility for yourself, for your life, for the goals you decide to pursue, and for what you do with your time.

One of the best books I've read on taking responsibility for your life is *Beyond Success and Failure* by

Willard Beecher and Marguerite Beecher. The core message of that book is that you—every one of us—must learn to be self-reliant. By self-reliant, the authors don't mean isolated, selfish, or unable to ask for help. They mean responsible for the choices we make in our lives. It's not a self-help book with a program or steps. It's a book about learning to become an adult, with all of the responsibilities and rights that implies.

Take Action

Read *Beyond Success and Failure: Ways to Self-Reliance and Maturity* by Willard Beecher and Marguerite Beecher (DeVorss & Company, 2003). By the way, this updated edition is superior to the original that was published back in the 1960s.

Everyone has dreams, but few people act on them. Everyone has things they'd love to be doing, but they're doing something else. I don't mean that they'd rather be fishing or skiing or knitting or any of the other bumper sticker sayings. I mean they would rather be doing different work, be living in a different place, or, in extreme cases, have different lives. But they believe that they have to do what they're doing, and live where they live and in the way they are living.

They will say, "I have to keep this job because I need the money," or "I have to live here because everyone I know is here." There's an old saying: "The only things you have to do are eat, sleep, and pay taxes."

I realize that we all have certain responsibilities—to spouses, children, and creditors—and that those responsibilities can lead us to feel boxed in. But I also realize that we can change a whole lot of things that we

THINGS YOU CAN CHANGE

- ○ *Job, profession, employer*

- ○ *Education, skills, interests*

- ○ *Marital status, religion, friends*

- ○ *Location, wardrobe, car, finances*

neu•ro•ses

1. commonly, failure to adjust to life's demands

2. more commonly, depression, anxiety, phobias, and other psychological issues

3. most accurately, problems or obstacles to doing good work and loving other people

often don't believe we can change. These include our line of work, level of education, skills, location, lifestyle, marital status, religion, friends, looks, wardrobe, car, and financial situation.

Yes, in making these changes you might displease, alienate, or hurt other people. I am not recommending that you do whatever you want and run roughshod over everyone. I am recommending that you consciously weigh the costs and benefits (to yourself and to those for whom you feel responsible) of various decisions. Often we feel that other people will fall apart if we change something or pursue something in our lives, when they wouldn't. Sometimes they would fall apart, if only temporarily, because of their neuroses, problems, dependencies, or unrealistic or unfair expectations. Sometimes they use the threat of falling apart to keep us from making changes.

When it comes to making decisions about your life, you have to take care of others but you also have to take care of yourself—

especially if you're living a life without real motivation.

So, What Do You Want?

Simple question, isn't it?

Well, not really. It's difficult for many of us to know what we want. This occurs for one or more of the following reasons:

> The consuming desire of most human beings is deliberately to plant their whole life in the hands of some other person. I would describe this method of searching for happiness as immature. Development of character consists solely in moving toward self-sufficiency.
> **—Quentin Crisp (author)**

- *Parents and other family members have dreams for us, push us in certain directions, or label or limit us in certain ways.*

- *Teachers, coaches, and school experiences create or reinforce certain ideas about what we can and can't do—or even want.*

- *Certain religions make moral judgments about perfectly legitimate desires and activities and foster skewed views about money, social usefulness, and aspirations.*

- *Cultural and commercial messages—and peer pressure—spread the idea that if we are not making or spending lots of money then we are not doing something worthwhile.*

○ *Celebrity worship fosters the idea that if
we're not famous, we lack value; there-
fore, we'd better aspire to be famous
whether or not we have any salable
talent that leads to fame.*

These and other messages pervade your world. We
all hear them from a very young age and we can see
their effects on people we know, and perhaps even on
ourselves. The question is, how do you think clearly
about what you really want?

The American Way?

In the United States today, people spend a high pro-
portion of their time and energy getting and spend-
ing. Americans spend more time working than their
European counterparts, and, when you look at our
consumer goods, automotive, and housing industries,
we have done more to elaborate what Maslow would
classify as basic needs. It's not only worth asking
whether or not this will lead to self-actualization, but
it's also worth asking if this emphasis on getting and
spending could get in the way of doing what we really
want to be doing with our lives.

Sally Edwards, author and founder of retail athletic
shoe chain Fleet Feet, put it this way in an interview I con-
ducted with her on the subject of working for yourself:

*The risks of pursuing an independent living are perceived
as very high for most people, but a lot of that perception*

flows from the entire American system of debt and responsibility and peer pressure. Really, you just have to decide what is important to you. I think that people should be who they are and not try to be what they are told they should be. But our entire system constantly tells people what they should be, and it takes a lot of strength to fight that.

These are not the words of a wild-eyed socialist revolutionary or a starry-eyed artist manqué but rather those of a triathlete and serial entrepreneur.

Where do you get "a lot of strength to fight that" system of debt, responsibility, and peer pressure? I have found studying role models to be one excellent method.

> **art•ist man•qué**
>
> 1. someone who could have become an artist, but did not
>
> 2. frustrated artist or artist who fails to realize his or her ambitions

The Value of Role Models

If you want to pursue a life of getting and spending, you face no shortage of role models. But what if you want to pursue an independent living, or become an artist or adventurer? You have to look a bit harder for role models, but they are out there.

In fact, whatever it is you want to do, someone has done it—or something very much like it. You don't need to meet your role models or see them in person, although that can be useful. You just have to know that they exist and know something about how they went about doing what they did. Those people help you motivate yourself because you see what's possible. You see that what you dream about has actually been done.

Take Action

Not to be morbid, but reading the obituaries in a good newspaper, not just those of famous people but also of accomplished but lesser-known executives, salespeople, teachers, inventors, and so on, can be enlightening and inspiring.

One of the things I love about newspapers and magazines is the sheer number of people they cover and the depth in which good journalists cover them. People enjoy talking about themselves and skilled interviewers ask questions that reveal the mental processes and the steps that the interview subjects took to get to where they are.

If you read about enough extraordinary people—and, whatever their faults, many of the people covered in the media are extraordinary—you begin to see patterns. I'm talking about the entrepreneurs, executives, politicians, performers, talent agents, sports stars, teachers, doctors, writers, and artists you learn about in the media. You begin to see patterns in the paths they took and in their personalities and values.

Here are a few things I've noticed that not every accomplished person you read about possesses, but many do:

They care about the activity itself. Yes, it's easy for successful people to say they didn't do it for the money—but you know?—I tend to believe them. Leaving the executives and entrepreneurs aside, there are much surer ways of making money than performing, sports, writing, or the arts—and most teachers and many doctors are motivated by the work and the opportunity to be useful rather than the earnings.

They follow their instincts. I'm often astonished to hear someone—including people I know personally—say, "I was never attracted to the nine-to-five grind," or "I never wanted to work for anyone else." Right, okay. But what made them think they could avoid it? Fact is, they never seriously considered nine-to-five or working for someone else as options, because those were against their instincts. So they had to find other ways of making their way in this world.

They were alive to opportunity. They sought out role models and teachers and were open to influence. They pursued the formal or informal education and the work they needed in order to gain the knowledge and experience and exposure they required. They traveled to places that offered the best chance of learning what they needed to know and of showcasing their talents. (I still can't figure out how Prince got started in Minneapolis.)

They judge themselves by their own standards, but they listen to feedback. Motivated people typically walk a thin line between listening

to themselves and listening to criti-
cism and advice. They have enough
ego strength to hear what they need
to hear in order to improve, while
ignoring criticism that's inaccurate or
unhelpful.

Watching role models can seem
like fantasizing unless you remember that most of
them are ordinary people who pursued what they
wanted with extraordinary energy and perseverance.
Yes, some are tremendously gifted and talented. But
even gifted, talented people have to show up for
work. No actor is right for every part. Few politicians
never lose a race. Most entrepreneurs and executives
have lost money, jobs, and opportunities. But they
believe in themselves.

You Gotta Believe

To believe that you have a good chance of produc-
ing a result, you have to believe you are doing the
right things and you have to believe in yourself. Doing
the right things has to do with knowledge and skill.
You can learn the basics of management, and even
the skills of the senior executive, such as leadership,
strategic thinking, negotiation, and communication.
But to use those skills to achieve something, you have
to believe in yourself.

What is belief in yourself? It's understanding that
you have something to offer to people—individu-
als, organizations, and the world—and that they

Two of My Role Models

It took me many years to pursue writing full time. As I found myself getting older, I found encouragement from two writers who began publishing books after their youth. One was James Michener, whose first book, *Tales of the South Pacific* (the inspiration for the Broadway show and movie *South Pacific*), was published when he was forty. Another was Frank McCourt, whose first book, *Angela's Ashes*, came out when he was sixty-four.

will accept it when you present it in the right way. It's also understanding that others have something to offer you, and being open to that. Most of all, it's the knowledge and feeling that you deserve to be in this world, deserve to act on your desires, and deserve to fulfill—or at least to pursue—your purpose and destiny. In other words, it's the belief that you deserve to be happy.

Do You Deserve to Be Happy?

A surprising number of people believe on some deep level that they do not deserve to be happy. They honestly believe that happiness, and the things that generate happiness, like engaging work, good relationships, enjoyable experiences, material comforts, and a good income are somehow, for some reason, not for them.

Am I saying that these things—work, relationships, experiences, comforts, and income—bring happiness? As a matter of fact, I am. Unrewarding work, troubled relationships, bad experiences, discomfort, and poverty cannot be viewed as a recipe for happiness. Of course, not everyone needs the same things in the same proportions in order to be happy. But most of us have certain needs in these areas and if those needs are not met, it's going to be hard to be happy.

Surveys on what makes people happy are inconclusive. I saw a report several years ago that definitely correlated higher income with greater happiness. I pointed this out to someone much older than I, and they said, "Of course. You have more freedom to do what you want to do." Other surveys have found that good relationships and health are more highly correlated with happiness than money is.

The point, however, is that some people don't seem to believe that they deserve to be happy, regardless of what would make them happy. This mental attitude, which in some cases may be related to clinical depression, can undercut motivation before you even start. It causes you to avoid considering your purpose, setting goals, or planning tasks. It prompts you to dismiss every dream or hope. Why? Because those things are for other people, people who are somehow more deserving.

Now I could tell you that as one of God's creatures you are meant to be happy and so on; but if you're determined to believe that you don't deserve happiness you may persist. However, I'm going to give it a try. Here are five reasons to believe that you deserve happiness:

1. You were born into a relatively good situation. Yes, other people may have nicer homes, more competent parents, better health, more wealth, or some other advantage. But if you're reading this, you are far, far better off than at least a few billion people in this world.

> Nature does nothing uselessly.
> —Aristotle (Greek philosopher)

2. Many people, including parents, teachers, and "friends" find satisfaction in undercutting others' senses of value and self-esteem. These people are miserable themselves due to personality disorders, psychological issues, immaturity, bitterness, or failure to do much with their own lives. Dismiss these people and their opinions. They are extremely small people.

3. The Declaration of Independence guarantees, in writing, your right to pursue happiness. While it doesn't guarantee the right to happiness, it does state that every person (not just Americans, come to think of it) has the unalienable right to life, liberty, and the pursuit of happiness.

4. Nature tends not to waste anything. If you were put on this earth, the way to bet is that it's to serve some purpose other than being a bad example. Find—or decide—what that purpose is, and decide to fulfill it.

5. You will deserve to be happy, and actually find some happiness, if you do something, anything, to make

this world a better place. There's so much negativity, misfortune, cruelty, and violence in this world that opportunities to improve it abound. Compliments, encouragement, acts of kindness, and even good manners really make a difference.

Discover Your Purpose, or Decide What It Is

After clearing away all of this social and psychological underbrush, you still have to do the work of discovering or deciding what your purpose will be in life—or at least over the next few years. Here are some guidelines and techniques:

- *Really consider your visions, dreams, fantasies, and idealized versions of your life; you think these things for a reason.*

- *Go toward what you're emotionally drawn to and avoid what turns you off; remember those people who say, "I was just never drawn to the nine-to-five grind."*

- *Consider the things that you really believe are important in this life, whatever they are; consider the things that you want to have and be and do regardless of whether you actually think these things are possible.*

- *Think about what you really have to offer this world; think about your real interests, skills, and talents and consider the ones that other people have pointed out to you.*

- *Remember that you can change your mind if you decide to follow a path that doesn't feel right next week or next year; that you can change your mind, but only if you first make up your mind.*

Your purpose or overall vision will guide you in the goals that you choose—so, while you shouldn't analyze it to death, do give it some thought.

" A GOAL IS A DREAM WITH A
DEADLINE.
"

—Napoleon Hill
(author)

6

Get Set for Success: Establishing Motivating Goals

Goals move you from the realm of dreams into reality. Goals focus your motivation on things you can achieve and obtain in the real world, as opposed to things you think that you would do if only the world, or you, were different. You set a goal, define the tasks that will move you toward that goal, and develop ways to get those tasks done. That brings things to the real-world level. This chapter covers the areas of your life in which you can set goals, and then brings them to the action level in the next two chapters.

Let's Break It Down

How do you look at your life? Do you see yourself as drifting along, doing what happens to be in front of you, taking the occasional suggestion, and going along to get along? Or do you have things defined a bit more sharply and Take Action more proactively? Many of us find we can make more sense of our lives by stepping back, looking things over, and breaking them down into phases and parts.

Basic phases include childhood, adolescence, young adulthood, adulthood, middle age, and old age. Many people see their lives this way. Others view their lives in ten- or twenty-year chunks. This can lend structure to something that can seem unstructured.

Structure helps when it guides you to make decisions that serve your vision and purpose. But if you find yourself panicking because you're somehow not conforming to certain expectations about these phases—for instance, if you're not married or having kids by a certain age, or if you're regretting that you got married and had children so young—then the structure may box you in or come crashing down on you. So use what works for you and what helps, and avoid anything that doesn't.

How I See It

When I was in college, I knew it couldn't last. I saw the responsibilities my parents faced, and prepared myself mentally, emotionally, and educationally to deal with them—later. In school I focused mainly on having fun. When the time came for earning a living, paying my bills, and running my own life, I was okay with it because I was prepared and I had already had a great time as a kid.

Functional Areas of Life

Now let's look at life in yet another way, in terms of functional areas. These are areas where you can really create goals. These are also ways to think about your life so you can see it clearly. When you see your life clearly you can explicitly decide what's important to you, what you want, how you're going to go about getting what you want, and how you will strike a balance among your competing wants and needs.

I see the key areas of life as relating to:

- *Work and profession*

- *Income and wealth*

- *Possessions and experiences*

- *Health and fitness*

- *Relationships and family*

These areas can help you organize your thinking, goals, time, and efforts. The emphasis that each of us places on an area is up to us, and it can vary at different times in our lives. For instance, when we're young most of us spend time socializing and developing relationships, seeking out experiences, and finding a career. Then, as we get older, most of us spend time growing professionally, building wealth, and caring for family. There are real tradeoffs to be made among these areas, but that's okay because not everyone has the same needs, nor can anyone do everything all the time.

Here's how I see these categories and why I think they're useful.

Work and Profession

Virtually everyone needs to work. Even people who don't need to work for financial reasons typically want to work. Work is our way of contributing our knowledge, energy, and skills to the world.

Notice that I've separated work from income and wealth. This may strike you as odd. After all, aren't we working for the money? Well, yes, but I separate the two because choosing a profession purely, or even mainly, on the basis of the money you think you'll make can be a mistake. Many people find that they not only enjoy life more, but also make more money by choosing work they really want to do, regardless of the money.

Multipreneuring

In the mid 1990s, I wrote a book called *Multipreneuring*. It was about using multiple skills, lines of work, and income streams to ensure that you can always make a living. I wrote it because many companies were laying off managers and professionals at the time, which led to "white collar unemployment." I wrote it while working full time, partly to motivate myself to find a way to earn an independent living and partly to start earning one.

Your choice of profession is important, but it's not set in stone, especially today. Most people now know that they can change professions, not to mention jobs, more easily than in the past. This is partly born of necessity, because changes in the economy and the job market now occur more frequently than in the past. In fact, many of us now must be ready, willing, and able to change jobs and even professions in order to continue to earn a living and have rewarding work.

Take Action
Check out *Multipreneuring* (Fireside/Simon & Schuster, 1996), which is out of print but still available from online booksellers such as Amazon (*www.amazon.com*) and Abe Books (*www.abebooks.com*).

Although you can change them, the professional goals you set for yourself have a huge impact on your life at the daily level and over the long term.

Income and Wealth

I separate income and wealth from work because you might choose work that's intellectually or emotionally satisfying, but not very lucrative. What do you do? Resign yourself to a life of poverty? Give up dreams that involve money?

No. You learn to manage your money in creative ways. You choose a lower cost geographical area or a less expensive housing arrangement—or both. But mainly you learn to save and invest, which even people with high incomes must do.

Also, income and wealth are two different things. They are both sums of money, but income is the sum of money that comes in (hence in come) every week, month, quarter, and year. It's a flow of money. Of course, income is accompanied by outgo—your ongoing and occasional outlays, including living expenses, unexpected costs, and celebratory splurges.

Over time, income minus outgo equals wealth. Wealth is a store of money, not a flow of money. It's a cache, if you will. A high income is a wonderful thing, but it's not being independently wealthy. You don't have to become independently wealthy to be happy. But in this world, few things offer as much freedom and security. Moreover, the older you grow, the more important it is to become independently wealthy.

It's absolutely essential for each of us to have financial goals and a plan for reaching them. Yet despite the importance of income and wealth in our lives—or perhaps because of it—many people lack motivation or fail to take action in this area. So we'll spend some time on motivation as it relates to your finances.

A Bit About Debt

Borrow only to finance the purchase of large assets, such as houses, co-ops, cars, or businesses. As long as you earn enough to repay the loan and live decently, debt isn't bad. But if you don't earn enough and you default on the loan, or if you borrow to finance restaurant meals, vacations, and rent payments, you can get into real trouble. It's good to have good credit, but you must use it wisely.

Possessions and Experiences

Possessions include your living quarters, car and other transportation, clothing, food, beverages, appliances, and so on. Alert readers will realize that most of these are what Abraham Maslow would call basic needs. However, as I pointed out, in a consumer society these needs have become elaborated into luxuries, badges of belonging, and forms of self-expression. There's nothing basic about a Mercedes.

Here is where many of us have to work hard to think for ourselves. If you aspire to own certain things, ask yourself why? Why do you want a certain car? Yes, a Porsche Boxster is more fun to drive than a Nissan Sentra. But can you really afford it? Is buying (or leasing) the Porsche going to undermine your goals in other areas of your life? Will you have to take on debt or work on weekends? Is that good? Or does it cut into your surfing, family, or museum-going time?

In a consumer culture permeated with advertising, it takes conscious thought and even willpower to decide what you're really motivated to buy, own, eat, drink, and drive, and to stick with it.

Regarding experiences, why do so many of us spend so many hours a week watching television and surfing the Web? Perhaps we're deficient in motivating ourselves to seek cultural and recreational experiences. If you think it's enough to hear recorded music, watch games on TV, and see works of art on the Web, then you haven't been to a concert, stadium, or museum lately. The upside of the technology revolution—that technology brings experiences to us—is also its

Make a Lifelong To-Do List

Everyone should have a list of things they want to do before they are called home, as the Quakers say. Want to go bonefishing in the Caribbean? See the pyramids? Live in New York, London, or Singapore? Cruise the Amazon? Swim the English Channel? Learn a foreign language? Set goals, get motivated, and think of ways to make it happen. You can revise your list occasionally. Just be sure to act on it.

downside. There's nothing like being there. I know some people who never even get out to a movie.

Which reminds me: Do you travel much? I've read that only about 15 percent of Americans have passports. Talk about not getting around. The Microsoft advertisement asked, "Where do you want to go today?" Try asking yourself that question with the intention of leaving your chair. Think about what you'd like to see, learn, hear, and do—and about ways to motivate yourself to seek out those things.

Take Action

If you've never read the mega bestseller by M. Scott Peck, M.D., *The Road Less Traveled* (Touchstone, second edition, 1998), be sure to do so. It's a wonderful meditation on how to live.

Health and Fitness

Ah, this area is where motivation is most difficult for many of us. First, let's distinguish between health and fitness. Health is freedom from disease, disorders, and most disabilities. I say most disabilities because a blind person has a disability but can still be healthy and physically fit. Physical fitness is the ability to function at a good, or better, level of physical performance for your age and in the activities you choose.

That last part gives rise to misunderstandings. What is fit "for your age," and which activities do you want to pursue? For a person who's been in a severe accident or who has had a stroke, "fitness" may mean the ability to perform the activities of daily living. For someone training for a marathon, fitness means the ability to run twenty-six miles in a competitive time. A lot of levels of fitness fall in between these two extremes, but the level you choose to pursue and maintain is up to you.

> ## ac•tiv•i•ties of dai•ly liv•ing
>
> 1. getting dressed, feeding yourself, bathing, using the bathroom, climbing stairs, and getting in and out of beds, chairs, and motor vehicles
>
> 2. also known as ADLs

As in many areas, social expectations, peer pressure, and various comparisons bedevil our notions of health and fitness and affect our motivation in this area, for better and worse. Advertising, movies, family, and friends—and a constant stream of health information—make it hard for many of us to think clearly here. However, thinking clearly is possible, and we'll examine ways of doing that in Chapter 8.

Relationships and Family

Most of us benefit tremendously from motivation and goal setting in this area. Why? Because most of us just let things happen rather than make things happen when it comes to our relationships. We become friends with the people we happen to meet instead of seeking out people we want to befriend. We always wait for someone else to make the first move. We take our loved ones for granted rather than trying to make their lives better every day.

Meanwhile, nothing is more important than our relationships. The strongest, deepest urge in most of us is the desire to love and be loved and to know and be known for who we are by someone we value. Social needs, esteem needs, safety needs, and procreative needs are all bound up in our relationships. Yet most of us conduct our relationships without giving them much thought, or at least not enough of the right kind of thought. Each of us can benefit by examining our relationships and setting goals in this area.

Big Deals

Goals and tasks that require you to be motivated are more complex and difficult than routine goals and tasks. Here are types and examples of goals and tasks that typically require large amounts of motivation:

> ○ *Attaining high professional stature, such as physician, attorney, certified public*

accountant, business owner, or senior executive

○ *Reaching a significant level of wealth, such as owning a multimillion dollar investment portfolio or a business that provides a dependable independent income*

○ *Completing a creative project such as a film, novel, painting, or other artistic achievement*

○ *Undertaking and completing a lengthy course of study for a diploma, degree, vocational training, or other intellectual accomplishment, such as mastering a foreign language or reading all of Shakespeare's plays*

○ *Tackling an athletic endeavor, such as running a marathon, finishing a bicycle race, climbing a mountain, or compiling a winning record in a competitive sport*

○ *Overcoming a physical or psychological challenge, such as surviving a serious accident, ending dependency on alcohol or drugs, or enjoying life despite a disability*

○ *Making permanent personal changes, such as improving your fitness or health, ending bad habits, changing your physical appearance (without surgery), or improving your relationships*

> People with goals succeed because they know where they are going. . . . It's as simple as that.
> —**Earl Nightingale** (entrepreneur and author)

In the next two chapters we'll see how to set specific goals and define tasks that will enable you to reach your goals in these areas. Now, however, I just want to delve a bit more deeply into why these goals and tasks present motivational difficulties.

What's the Problem?

These goals and tasks require motivation because they:

- *They take a long time.*

- *They require new skills.*

- *They demand hard work and change.*

- *They present the possibility of failure.*

- *They call for you to invest in yourself.*

How to Set Motivating Goals

Make the goal desirable. I need not belabor this—set goals that you really, really want to achieve. Don't pretend that you want to achieve them or adopt goals that someone else wants you to achieve. Adopt only goals that you really want to achieve.

Make the goal challenging but achievable. If the goal doesn't stretch your capabilities, how will it keep you motivated? On the other hand, if it's beyond your capabilities and time horizon, you'll be frustrated and want to give up.

Break the goal into subgoals. For instance, if you want to spend a year or two living abroad, think about what it's going to take. How about scheduling some visits? How about learning about the culture and people? How much of the language can you learn? Will you rent, buy a home, live in a hotel, or swap homes with someone? Where can you find a magazine for expatriates or meet some expats to learn how they did it?

Write your goals down and refer to them often. We've all heard this, but few of us do it. I can tell you that whenever I've had written goals, it has always helped. Some people think they "can't write," which has nothing to do with it. Others think they don't need written goals because they already know them. But you don't write down your goals because you don't know them. You write them down to clarify them and because writing something down makes it more real to you. It's no longer just in your head; it's now on paper or in your computer.

" **THE REASON MOST PEOPLE NEVER REACH THEIR GOALS** IS THAT THEY DON'T DEFINE THEM, LEARN ABOUT THEM, OR EVEN SERIOUSLY CONSIDER THEM AS BELIEVABLE OF ACHIEVEMENT. "

—Denis Waitley
(motivational speaker
and author)

7

Pursuing Professional Goals

In this chapter we are going to examine your professional and financial life and then, in Chapter 8, your personal life. We're not starting with your professional and financial life because it's more important—it actually isn't. We're starting with that area because it's easier for most of us to think about setting goals and defining tasks in those areas.

Work and money are related, of course, which is another reason we deal with them together. But again, I recommend that you think of work and wealth separately. Lots of people in relatively low-paying, unglamorous lines of work achieve financial independence through regular saving and wise investing. In this chapter we'll look at setting motivating professional and financial goals and defining tasks that will move you toward those goals.

Professional Goals and Tasks

Your career goals should reflect your values and your purpose in life. If they don't, you may find yourself dealing with real internal conflict. For instance, if you believe that one of your purposes is to make enough money to support your family and you find yourself failing to fulfill that purpose, you may be setting yourself up for real difficulty. Was that a reasonable purpose for you, or not?

So as in all areas, knowing yourself and being honest with yourself are extremely important. In other words, consider what you find most motivating—the things you want to obtain or achieve and the timeframes for achieving them. If you want higher earnings or greater autonomy, you may be able to achieve these things in a senior executive position, in your own business, or in a new career. Then you set long-term and interim goals and define tasks that you must perform to get you there.

Professional goals can be framed in any way that works for you and then be organized into a career plan. Here are some general guidelines for setting goals and defining tasks that will move you toward them:

SYSTEMATIC SUCCESS

- *Your purpose sets the context.*

- *Goals serve your purpose.*

- *Tasks are things you do to move toward your goals.*

- *Include one-, two-, five-, ten-, and twenty-year goals, and lifetime goals.*

- Break one-year goals and the related tasks into quarterly, monthly, and weekly goals and tasks.

- Distinguish between major goals and interim goals. Major goals are significant milestones, states of being, positions, and situations. Interim goals are milestones, states, and positions on the way to major goals.

- Distinguish between goals, which are destinations, and tasks, which are activities.

So, major goals break down into interim goals. You work on tasks and complete them in order to reach interim goals, and you use certain skills and disciplines to work on the tasks. To perform the tasks you must have, acquire, or otherwise obtain the skills, for instance by hiring or partnering with someone who has them.

Open Up Your Thinking

When you consider a goal and the tasks required to achieve it, keep an open mind. It's easy to see a goal and only a few ways of reaching it, when in fact there may be myriad ways. One way to avoid getting boxed in is to define your goal broadly. For example, after I'd worked for companies for a few years and realized that (a) I wanted to work for myself and (b) I enjoyed writing more than anything else, my goal became to make my living as a freelance writer.

But here's how I usually framed things before I opened up my thinking: "Freelance writing doesn't pay as well as my salary as a middle manager in a *Fortune* 500 company, and I can't afford to (and don't want to) take a big pay cut. So I don't see how I can become a freelance writer."

After a while, I reframed my goal to be: to make my living by writing. That way, even if I couldn't become self-employed, I would at least be doing work I enjoyed and was good at, and, I reasoned, if I got good enough at it I could then perhaps go out on my own.

Goals Define Tasks, and Tasks Define Skills

Once I decided to make my living by writing, my major goals became:

To land a job as an editor or writer. I decided I would work as a writer or editor even if it was not at a publication; for instance, most large companies and consulting firms have internal writers and editors who work on the companies' materials and customer deliverables. It might have meant a pay cut or less responsibility for few years, but I would plan for and deal with that.

Or:

To begin my own freelance writing business. I originally didn't envision writing books but rather freelance marketing communications, such as sales letters, brochures, and product literature. I had a marketing background and believed I could leverage that to win assignments in that area.

Given these two goals, I defined several tasks:

1. To gain more on-the-job writing experience.

2. To be published in an actual publication.

3. To get freelance writing work, even if not for publication.

The skills I needed to develop included:

○ *Writing skills*

○ *Typing skills*

○ *Knowledge of the job market*

These are just a few examples of the tasks and skills I defined. Of course, if I'd wanted a job in advertising or a career in arts management, I would have defined a different set of goals and tasks and required different skills.

Here is a general method of setting professional goals and defining tasks:

Set Goals: Set a few long-term and shorter-term goals; for instance, your ultimate goal may be to have your own advertising agency or

Caution: Exploitation Ahead!

If you're motivated by a job, that's great, but don't let anyone exploit that fact. I'm not telling you to hang back. You will usually get in keeping with what you give, but not always. For instance, insist that your vacation time is vacation time. You need that time to recharge and to perform well on the job. Plus, it's part of your compensation!

accounting practice, but you first have to learn the business, enter the business in some capacity, experience several facets, see where you fit, learn the economics of the business, and gain some real expertise.

Define tasks: Learn how to enter the trade and get hired, including any licensing and apprenticeship requirements; obtain formal and informal education, perhaps at a trade school, on-the-job, or both; learn what leads people to succeed (and fail) in the business; discover and develop your strengths and compensate for your weaknesses; find the route that people take to become practitioners or entrepreneurs in these areas—and the route that will work for you.

ap•pren •tice•ship

1. formal or informal period of training under an experienced practitioner

2. requirement for licensing in certain trades and professions

Thinking about Income and Wealth

As important as money is, many of us don't give it enough thought—or at least not enough of the right kind of thought. We worry, or we don't worry. We obsess, or we forget about it. We read about budgeting and investing, and then don't act on it. We follow fads, such as day trading or investing in dot-com companies or real estate, and then wonder why we got burned.

Useful thinking about money is rooted in three things:

1. The right attitude toward money.

2. The right information about money and wealth building.

3. The right habits regarding money management.

The Right Attitude Toward Money

Money is an emotionally charged issue for many of us. Perhaps it shouldn't be that way, since money is merely a way of measuring the relative value of goods and services in an economy. But several factors skew our views about money, including the following:

○ *The Protestant work ethic holds that people who work hard will see their* "virtue" rewarded in this life in terms of economic prosperity.

- In the United States in particular, many people view financial success as a reflection of energy, intelligence, and hard work—and lack of financial success as evidence of the absence of those things.

- Some religions and cultures view money as evil and people who have a lot of it as corrupt; many people are taught that any strong desire for money is a sin.

- People often use their economic power to reward or punish other people by giving or withholding money and the things it can buy; this occurs in families, communities, and on the national and international levels.

- The amount of money one earns is not always correlated with the value that people create in society; for instance, drug dealers and people who sell life-threatening but legal products, such as cigarettes and guns, typically earn more than teachers.

Take Action

For good information on changing your attitudes toward money, read *Your Money or Your Life* by Joe Dominguez and Vicki Robin (Penguin, 1999).

Money is just a tool. As you learned in basic economics, it is a medium of exchange. As teachers of those courses never tire of telling

Don't Just Watch

Often people who don't have much money avoid dealing with the money they do have. They don't create budgets, balance their checkbooks, save regularly, or plan major expenses. They don't deal with their money actively. Instead, they watch passively as it comes in and goes out, as if it were the weather. Money management is not a spectator sport.

us, it does away with the need for us to carry around chickens, bread, gasoline, and bales of cotton in order to engage in barter. As a tool and a medium of exchange, money operates by certain principles and behaves mainly in predictable ways. You can learn how money behaves and deal with it accordingly.

The Right Information About Money

There's no shortage of information about money. If anything, there's too much. The key thing is to get good, basic information.

When I say information about money I mean two things: First, I mean information about how to earn it, save it, invest it, and spend it wisely. Second, I mean information about your money—how much you have, where it comes from, where it goes, whether it could be working harder for you, and so on.

You need both kinds of information. You need to know how to make a budget, and you need to draw up a budget and stick with it. You need to know how

111

to save money—that is, the techniques that work for you—and you need to know how much you have saved. You need basic information about the savings and investment vehicles that will work for you, and you need to know how yours are performing. These topics are beyond the scope of this book, which is about how to get motivated to do these things.

Four Ways to Save Regularly

1. Use automatic payroll deductions so you don't see the money.
2. Cut yourself a monthly check when you pay your bills.
3. Reduce spending in a specific area, and save that amount monthly.
4. Contribute the maximum to any matching plan your employer operates.

Money and Goals

Building wealth requires that you set goals in two areas: earning money and managing money. Many people who are good at earning money actually have little interest in managing it. They make a good salary, but they don't build wealth because they live beyond their means.

Living beyond our means is a major problem—for many individuals and for the United States as a nation—so let's look at it. Living beyond your means is the act of spending more than you make. You do that by taking on debt. Living beyond your means is also spending everything you earn. If you spend everything you can never save, and if you don't save you will have to work all the time, through illnesses and old age, until you die. If you go through a period of unemployment or slow business, you will go into debt or lose valuable assets, such as your car, house, or business.

I've said that you should always try to set goals that are specific and measurable. That's relatively easy to do with income and wealth because money itself is a measure. For instance, any of the following would be reasonably stated financial goals:

- *To be earning X dollars annually and have net worth of Y dollars by age Z.*

- *To be completely debt-free and to own my home free and clear by age fifty-five.*

- *To be independently wealthy in twenty-five years.*

These are all valid ways of expressing financial goals, but the first one is the best because it specifies a dollar amount of earnings and net worth by a specific age. After you have defined the major goal or goals, it's essential to chart interim goals. These can be amounts that you must earn, save, and invest on an annual, quarterly, monthly, and even weekly basis. This is essential because those shorter-term, interim goals will help you become and remain motivated to do the tasks you must do to reach your financial goals.

WEALTH-BUILDING TASKS

- *Learn about money and how money works for people who save and invest it rather than just work for it.*

- *Make a yearly, quarterly, and monthly game of budgeting and understand that it is decision making, not a form of torture.*

- *Always know where your money is going—know how much of your money you are spending on which items and expenses.*

- *Save and invest regularly; when you realize a windfall, invest most or all of it.*

- *Set realistic targets for your investments and monitor their progress against those targets.*

- *Avoid get-rich-quick schemes like the plague—they only enrich those who run them.*

- *Develop the "gratitude attitude" of prosperity consciousness by tipping well and giving generously to charity.*

Remember that motivation often comes down to a conflict between instant gratification and delayed gratification. Two areas of life present this conflict in the starkest terms—one is

Take Action
Read *The Millionaire Next Door* by Thomas J. Stanley and William D. Danko (Pocket Books, 1998) for a look at how people really build wealth.

health and fitness, and the other is wealth building. You must think deeply and often about your spending decisions. What are you really doing when you spend your money? You are deciding to trade your hard work, the yield of your labor, energy, time, and intelligence, for whatever it is you are getting.

Ask yourself: Is this item, experience, subscription, meal, or whatever, worth the effort it took me to earn this money? Don't ask: Is it worth the money? Money is too symbolic; it's at a remove from your labor. If you're handing over a credit card, it's an even more symbolic real exchange.

Also really think about the alternative uses—especially the later alternative uses—for the money you are about to spend. How about a co-op in your favorite vacation destination? How about taking a year off from work down the road to live abroad or undertake a major creative project? How about health care, and maybe an extra measure of independence and dignity, in your old age?

Motivation very often comes down to making a conscious decision. Always remember that motivation is not just a feeling—it's also a decision. The feeling alone won't carry you all the way. It's the feeling along with the decision to act in a certain way that make it motivation.

The Right Habits

Forming the right habits about money takes discipline if you didn't form them when you were growing up. The key habits are:

Getting good deals on purchases. On major deals you have to comparison shop, patronize reputable sellers, and understand that the cheapest isn't always the best deal.

Avoiding negative cash flow. When you have to economize, do it fast. Also, don't waste time feeling bad about a setback.

Regular saving and investing. Over time regular savings add up to large sums, but the sooner you start the more you'll have when you are older.

Having a budget and sticking to it. You have a budget so that you know where your money is going and control where it goes.

Take Action
For hundreds of hints on frugal living, see Amy Dacyczyn's book *The Complete Tightwad Gazette* (Villard, 1998).

Some authors and observers see a huge plot afoot to keep Americans on the consumer treadmill and in debt. I don't see it as a plot—just as the American way of capitalism, in which advertisers push the idea of constant spending as the road to happiness. Counter to this, however, there is a low-key "frugal living movement" afoot as well. Frugal living means jumping off the consumer treadmill, not buying everything you see. It means forgetting about keeping up with the Joneses and, if it helps, even moving to a new neighborhood well away from them.

> Never keep up with the Joneses. Drag them down to your level.
> —**Quentin Crisp (author)**

"

MANY PERSONS HAVE A WRONG IDEA OF WHAT CONSTITUTES **TRUE HAPPI-NESS**. IT IS NOT ATTAINED THROUGH SELF-GRATIFICATION BUT THROUGH FIDEL-ITY TO A WORTHY PURPOSE.

"

—Helen Keller (author)

8
Pursuing Personal Goals

In this chapter we examine setting goals and defining tasks in the areas in your life apart from your profession and finances. These areas amount to your personal life—possessions and experiences, health and fitness, and relationships and family—and are areas where many of us either don't set goals or find them particularly difficult to achieve.

There are reasons for that. It's easy for many of us to think mainly about work and money, and to think that those are the only areas where we need motivation. Some people don't seem to need a lot of motivation in their personal lives; they just seem to have terrific marriages and friendships and personal interests that enrich their lives without exerting much effort. The rest of us, however, generally benefit from getting motivated and working on our personal lives. This chapter examines ways of doing that.

Possessions and Experiences

Possessions and experiences represent a huge part of your lifestyle. I'm defining this area to include where you live, what you drive and wear, and your interests and pursuits outside of your job, including the way you spend your leisure time and vacations.

Should you set goals and define tasks in these areas? It's up to you. Of course, most of us devote serious thought and planning to where we live and what we live in, and to our car and other major purchases. Many of us also put serious thought into our wardrobes. But the rest of our lives often comes down to what's on television or on the Web.

Of course, when it comes to goals related to possessions, most of us require very little coaching. Most of us know where we want to live, what we want to drive and wear, and so on. We typically need minimal education about our choices. The real goals—and tasks—in obtaining possessions relate to budgeting the money and shopping wisely.

But although possessions, experiences, and lifestyle are bound up with the amount of money you earn and have, I would say this: Many of us ignore low-cost experiences that could make our lives much richer. I'm not talking only about walking in the rain, gazing at sunsets, and howling at the moon, as wonderful as those pastimes are. I'm also talking about reading, going to inexpensive but interesting ethnic restaurants, getting involved in your community, and so on.

I'm talking about developing a real understanding of some of the better things in life: good music, art, literature, architecture, philosophy, and so on. Many people know something on the surface—food, wine, art, music, books—but don't make the effort to know it

> The time you enjoy wasting is not wasted time.
> **—Bertrand Russell (British philosopher)**

deeply. It actually takes effort, and you can set goals and define tasks in these cultural pursuits just as you can elsewhere.

Turn Off and Log Off

Many of us allow our lifestyles and experiences to happen to us. To become motivated to do something other than TV viewing or Web surfing, you must do something else. Here is where the action can truly create the mood. It's also where sitting around waiting for motivation or inspiration can be particularly futile.

I understand the joy of wasting time, and have been aware of the need for downtime most of my life. However, I've found that wasting time by lying around, napping, or gazing out the window can be the most satisfying way of all to do it, perhaps because it involves no commercial messages.

Let the Spirit Move You

While I only touch on the spiritual dimension of life in this book, I recognize that it's an essential element for many of us. It's also a very personal one, and one in which I happen to believe that setting goals— beyond those of treating other people as well as you can—may be a bit odd. Spiritual goals are of course legitimate, but they tend to be extremely difficult to measure, unless you are simply counting the hours you spend in prayer or worship, which isn't always the same as spiritual development.

Most of the people I know who have or have had spiritual goals measure their progress mainly by the way they feel—peaceful or not, close to God or not, accepting or not—and typically feel that they fall terribly short of their goals. Yet there's no question that there's a spiritual path to chart and travel in this life, if one chooses, and it requires tremendous motivation.

Health and Fitness

If you stop and think about it, it's strange that we would spend time wondering about our motivation to become healthy and fit. We all want to look good in our clothes—and out of them. We all want to live a long and healthy life. And we all want to be able to run for a train or plane, play with our kids, and hit the dance floor without keeling over. So what's the problem?

One problem is our taste buds—not the fact that we have them, but that we've trained them to crave sugar, salt, and fat. We've also trained our bodies to crave carbohydrates of a certain type.

Now before you throw this book across the room, please know that I

Take Action
Two books that I've found to be useful spiritual guides are *Zen Mind, Beginner's Mind* by Shunryu Suzuki (Weatherhill, 1973; Shambalya, 2006) and the Christian-focused *Celebration of Discipline* by Richard J. Foster (HarperSanFrancisco 20th anniversary editon, 1998).

Reaching Out

I recently attended the funeral of a neighbor who died young. The outpouring of gratitude for his life among his family and others who had known him well was deeply moving. As a full-time professor of computer science, Jim was as busy as anyone. But he'd spent many hours counseling students independently, working with his church's youth group, and coaching youth league sports. These things made a huge difference to those young people.

am not a health nut. I'm a fellow soldier fighting the battle of the bulge, getting to the gym three times a week, having a few drinks a week and the occasional plate of baby back ribs.

But I've gotten out of the habit of eating bacon, chips, fries, butter, ice cream, and many of the other salt, sugar, and fat bombs the food and restaurant industries hurl at us—except occasionally. Over the past year, I stopped drinking juices with high fructose corn syrup when I learned what a large source of calories they are. The only candy I eat is good chocolate. Yet I, too, have my Achilles tendon: I love cheese, and must fight that craving every day.

So what's my motivation?

As I said at the start of this section, basically, I want to look as good as I can, age as gracefully I can, be reasonably fit, and not court serious illness. Those motivations are close to universal. But we have to make them personal and shorter-term.

Focus on Short-Term Positives

Here's what works for me:

Like most people, I like short-term gratification. But I eventually found that I could learn to dislike the heavy, bloated, run-down feeling I get after a heavy meal. I learned to enjoy the near-term feeling of lightness and easy digestion that occurs after a reasonably sized meal of reasonably healthy ingredients.

I also find information to be motivating. I don't seek out much information on diet and health, but you can't get away from it. It's in many of the magazines I read, all of the newspapers, and lots of Web sites.

It is also possible, I've found, to retrain your taste buds. If you get into the habit of eating salad, fruit, yogurt, vegetables, and fish, you actually begin to like it. Fried food starts to taste heavy. Buffalo wings can start to seem gross.

So the short-term gratification becomes the fact that you like what you're eating. Does this sound like an idealized version of reality?

It's not. I am a big believer in acquired tastes. Here are two examples from my own life: When I first tasted sushi, I was baffled and bummed. The texture was weird and the taste was as bland as most fish I'd eaten. But over time I became a fan of sushi. The other example is scotch, which tasted like medicine when I first tried it. I had been a bourbon drinker, but a bartender told me that scotch is the best stuff you can drink if you drink liquor; he said I should just drink it exclusively for a few weeks. I did and, sure enough, he was right. After I became a scotch drinker, bourbon tasted like medicine.

Yet the point here has nothing to do with sushi or scotch, although, believe it or not, they go well together. (This is not a joke.) The point has to do with acquired tastes. Since then, I've acquired a taste for jazz, modern art, regular exercise, green vegetables, and most fruit. I am not about to tell you that a person can acquire a taste for anything, though maybe you can. I can't. Despite repeated attempts, I haven't acquired a taste for raw tofu (too bland), classical music (too square), or winter weather (too cold). But to each his own.

For your health and fitness, I highly recommend that you acquire some non-fattening, body-improving tastes, or what are known as positive addictions. In fact, positive addictions are recognized as an actual phenomenon. You don't experience actual, full-blown withdrawal if you don't keep up with a positive addiction. However, you might not feel as good as you normally do if you miss a few days.

Get Moving

I don't have to tell you about the benefits of exercise. You've heard about them, read about them, and probably experienced them. The question is, how do you motivate yourself to just do it?

Here's what's worked for me:

Thinking long term. Instead of trying to lose X pounds or reaching waist size Y by a certain date,

I adopted the short-term goal of just getting to the gym three or four times a week and the long-term goal of making exercise as much a part of my routine as taking out the trash and gassing up my car. That worked for me.

Not judging what I'm doing. Judgment and criticism are demotivating—so why do that to yourself? Getting the habit is more important than getting fast results.

Making it as convenient as possible. The single most important thing for me has been how close the gym is to my office. I'm now in an office that is literally two doors away from the gym. Talk about doing away with excuses.

Reveling in the aftereffects. Exercise feels great—when it stops. I've heard of people who enjoy the actual exercise, but I understand that mainly in the abstract. It's the aftereffect of relaxation that most of us enjoy.

Relationships and Family

A character in the existentialist philosopher Jean Paul Sartre's play *No Exit* famously said, "Hell is other people." Most of us know what he's talking about, especially if we've worked with the general public. But being without other people can be an even deeper hell.

Friendship has been celebrated throughout the centuries in fiction and in fact. I believe that everyone benefits from real friendships. By real friendships, I mean relationships in which people genuinely value and care about one another for who they are, and can talk with one another openly about their problems and dreams.

Setting Goals and Defining Tasks

There's a huge amount of personal chemistry involved in real friendships, and in any romantic relationship. That means it's practically impossible to make someone a true friend or make someone fall in love with you if they are not somehow predisposed to doing so. You can't make someone feel something for you that they don't or can't or won't feel.

This creates huge amounts of trouble, because personal attraction—in friendship and in romance—can be a one-way street. Or the degrees of attraction or interest can vary. Or, even more astonishing, you can both feel an intense attraction and interest only to have it fade away in a matter of weeks, months, or years.

It's a wonder anyone becomes friends or remains in love. But we do. I feel, as do many people, that if you have a few true friends and one or two true loves in your life, you're doing pretty well.

> **fam•i•ly of or•i•gin**
>
> 1. the family you were born into, and see at Thanksgiving
>
> 2. a source of difficulties that surface even in adult sons, daughters, and siblings

Family Ties

Here's how I think about my family, whether it's my family of origin (I'm the eldest of six children) or my wife and two sons: Whatever their faults and shortcomings, no one will ever know me as well, nor will I ever know anyone as well, and I'll never be as close to anyone nor will anyone ever be as close to me, as my family.

I see family as the closest set of relationships you will have, which is why they are the most difficult. The family you grew up in helped you forge your view of the world and many of your responses to it, and your ways of thinking, coping, and operating in social situations. If you start a family of your own you start another set of extremely close and potentially difficult relationships. The more aware you are of the effect of your own upbringing on your way of viewing the world and interacting with people, the better.

Loving Detachment

Many psychologists tell reasonable people who have troubled families of origin to develop "loving detachment" toward family members. You love them, but you maintain enough emotional distance to avoid the unreasonable demands, difficulties, and drama that such families generate. Love alone leaves you too vulnerable. Detachment alone renders you too remote. Loving detachment enables you to feel for and think about your family at the same time.

Relationships Take Work

Once you are in one, of course, close relationships do take work. Here are the kinds of goals that people who work at relationships typically set:

Take Action
To learn about codependency, visit *www.nmha .org/go/codependency* within the Web site for Mental Health America.

- To help the other person to feel secure, respected, and valued

- To support the other person in their purpose and goals

- To operate as a team rather than as combatants

- To retain a sense of autonomy within the relationship

Here are the kinds of tasks that people set for themselves to achieve these goals:

- Listen to the other person and see things from their perspective as well as from your own.

- Understand and consider the other person's feelings and needs.

au•ton•o•my

1. sense of worth and value apart from your role in a relationship

2. ability to decide and act without the other party's permission

129

- *Support the other person by being there for them when things get rough.*

- *Express your feelings to the other person and let them know your needs rather than expecting them to read your mind or anticipate your every need.*

- *Talk about the goals, plans, people, and situations in your lives, and work together to make good things happen.*

ADVANCED MOTIVATION

" THE PROBLEM IS NOT THAT THERE ARE PROBLEMS. **THE PROBLEM IS EXPECTING OTHERWISE AND THINKING THAT HAVING PROBLEMS IS A PROBLEM.** "

—Theodore Isaac Rubin
(psychiatrist)

9 Recovering Lost Motivation

If you think back to our discussion of the reasons that you need motivation and why it's an issue at all, you'll recall that it's needed because the goals are large, important, difficult, and usually long term. Those things represent challenges. So you need to be motivated to continue pursuing the goal, carrying out the tasks, and engaging in the behaviors. Or you need to adjust your goals or tactics.

The trouble in these situations is that you can lose your motivation along the way. The reasons for this vary, but you can almost always regain it. The only exceptions are when you should actually stop putting out continued effort in a particular direction. That involves rethinking your goals—perhaps even changing them—and considering changes in your approach to achieving them.

But even to be able to do that, you must first recover your motivation. To recover your motivation you typically have to overcome discouragement, and see your situation clearly enough to be able to chart a path forward. In this chapter we'll examine ways of doing that along with other forms that lost motivation can take, and what to do about it.

Forms of Lost Motivation

Lost motivation manifests itself in various ways, but I boil them down to three broad phenomena: discouragement, burnout, and obsession. Note that this chapter covers lost motivation. You were motivated to pursue something, you were pursuing it, and now you don't feel motivated to pursue it anymore. You may still be pursuing it, but you're aware that you're going through the motions rather than pursuing it with real motivation.

Recovering your motivation to pursue or achieve something differs from developing motivation in the first place. When you're developing initial motivation you're doing so for the first time, for the first time in a while, or for the first time on a certain endeavor. You're psyching yourself up, getting pumped, and gathering and directing your energy.

When you've lost your motivation, it's a matter of regaining it, which differs from having to develop it in the first place. You know what it's like to be motivated, and you can find a way to recapture it if the goal is still important to you. In that way, recovering motivation is easier than developing it in the first place.

Yet in another way, it's more difficult. As in many areas of life, sustaining motivation differs from the initial spark of enthusiasm and burst of energy that accompanies the beginning of an endeavor. Sustaining something requires work,

Take Action
Go to *www.quotations page.com/mqotd.html* for a few motivational quotes that change every day.

diligence, and at times sheer willpower. (Think of marriage as opposed to the wedding, and pregnancy as opposed to—well, you get my drift.)

You often lose motivation when you discover that you have propelled your dreams and plans into a brick wall. Dreams and plans reside inside you; making them real means dealing with the real world. The real world can be tough, even heartless. Translating dreams and plans into reality takes hard work in the world of hard facts and sometimes even harder people, with the limited resources of time, money, and energy.

So, even with the most motivating goals and diligent execution of your plan, you can find yourself unable to sustain your motivation. Here's how to deal with it.

When You're Discouraged

There's a terrific line in the sentimental but very well-done classic Christmas film *It's a Wonderful Life*. When Clarence, the angel who must earn his wings on that Christmas Eve, is told by the head angel, Franklin, that his big case is going to be George Bailey, Clarence asks, "Is he sick?" Franklin replies, "No, worse. He's discouraged."

Franklin sees being discouraged as worse than being sick. As people examining motivation, we should

Ups and Downs

Many wise people have pointed out that things are never as good or as bad as we make them out to be. When we are up and enthusiastic, we're probably being overly optimistic, and when we are down and discouraged, we're probably being overly pessimistic. This has been my experience, and I try to bear it in mind on both the upswings and downswings—but more on the downswings.

feel the same. Discouragement isn't the opposite of motivation. Lack of motivation is the opposite of motivation. But discouragement undermines motivation by causing you to doubt the validity of your goals, your ability to reach them, and even yourself. Discouragement can lead to even worse things, such as depression or despair. Discouragement generally involves frustration, anger, or blame—often directed toward yourself—over setbacks, barriers, delays, or actual failure.

When you're discouraged in your pursuit of a goal you need to set aside your emotions—remember that discouragement is an emotion—and examine the matter calmly, rationally, and analytically. There are also things you can do to address discouragement from the emotional standpoint. This starts with how you communicate with yourself when you're discouraged.

Listen to Yourself

Each of us holds a running conversation with ourselves in our heads, and the quality of that conversation affects our motivation. Pep talks can be useful, but when you've lost your motivation—when you're discouraged, burned out, or obsessing—hold off on the pep talks until you know what's going on. To know what's going on, listen to yourself.

Discouraged people talk in terms of how bad things are, how bad they, themselves, are, and how bad other people are. Talk about how bad things are sounds like this:

"This is hopeless. It's never going to work. I'm so far behind, so off course, and so deep in the hole that I'll never catch up, get back, or climb out."

These are examples of what Dr. Albert Ellis calls "awfulizing." (I mentioned Dr. Ellis and his Rational Emotive Behavior Therapy in Chapter 4.) Awfulizing is telling yourself how incredibly awful your situation is in various ways. Some people talk this way all the time, but it's endemic among the discouraged. Discouragement is the opposite of enthusiasm, and when you're discouraged it's natural to paint a dark picture; but that picture will rarely be entirely accurate.

Discouraged people often blame themselves for setbacks, barriers, and failures. But blaming yourself is different from taking responsibility, mainly because the agenda with blame is to make yourself feel bad rather than to figure out what part of the situation you "own" (the decisions) and what part you don't own (the occurrences). Blaming yourself sounds like this:

"I was totally stupid. I was a fool to try this. How could I have been such a jackass? How could I have not seen it coming? I waited way too long to face up."

137

Sometimes this kind of talk echoes things we were told as children. Or we say them to beat real or imagined critics to the punch. Unfortunately, blaming yourself makes you feel worse about an already tough situation, and obscures your view of it. Blanket blame can blind you to what you really did do incorrectly, so that you repeat the mistake down the road. Self-blame can become a lifelong habit that separates people from accomplishment and success, so it's behavior to be avoided.

Sooner or later, many discouraged people get around to blaming someone else for their troubles on the path to achievement.

"That guy really ripped me off. He didn't do anything he said he would. I've got to get that SOB into court. Or maybe sugar his gas tank!"

Blaming other people can feel good. We get angry and curse and swear because venting in that way gives us a sense of power and control. If only it solved the problem. Alas, it doesn't. So if you want to throw a fit, go ahead—but don't think for a moment that it's going to solve anything.

Dealing with Discouragement

The word "discouraged" clearly points to the problem: Someone who is discouraged lacks courage because something has diminished his or her courage. Discouraged is to courage as disempowered is to empowered and disappear is to appear. Again, to recover your courage you have to see reality clearly.

First Task: Coolly Face Reality

Believe it or not, being discouraged can be a good thing. It's quite likely a sign that you are seeing the situation clearly. You perceive a gap or shortcoming between your efforts and your results, your goals and your achievements. To perceive that is the first step toward dealing with the actual problem.

If you are failing to make progress or are somehow falling short of your goals or timetable, perhaps your goals or timetable were too ambitious, or you have been doing the wrong things or doing the right things in the wrong way. To see this is good. What's not good is to think that you are on the right track and making progress when you are not.

What If You Didn't Do Your Best?

If you must admit to yourself that you didn't do your best, you have another line of inquiry to follow:

- *Why didn't you do your best?*

- *Do you care as deeply about the goal as you originally thought?*

- *Did you hold back from putting out your best effort? If so, why?*

- *What would you differently next time?*

- *Did you fear success, failure, rejection, or criticism?*

- *Where do you go from here?*

This kind of analysis is usually best performed with a pen and paper or at a computer. Writing about this sort of thing helps because you get it out of your head, where it tends to go in circles, and into a medium where you can see your thoughts expressed. I know I'm a writer and that's easy for a writer to say, but I did it when I was a garden-variety manager and business person, years before I was a writer. The discipline of writing helps you think more clearly.

Finally, don't rule out bad luck or others' mistakes or dishonesty. It's not the first thing to look for, but those factors can contribute to or even cause setbacks and failures. Just figure out what to do from where you are now, and how to avoid bad luck, incompetence, or dishonesty in the future.

Look at Progress, Not Just Gaps

Discouragement often comes about from the sheer length of time it can take to achieve a major goal. Indeed, when you read about people who've achieved something major, such as building a business or completing a feature-length film, they often say that if they had known how long it was going to take and how difficult it would be, they never would have undertaken the endeavor.

When you look at the effort, time, and money you have invested in something, and judge the goal to be still beyond the visible horizon, try this:

- *Think about what you would have been doing otherwise; yes, maybe you would now be the president of a university, but perhaps you would just have logged a lot more hours of TV viewing.*

- *Tote up the things that you've learned about the field and about yourself; you learn a lot more from the process than from the achievement.*

- *Consider the progress you have made. Yes, you may have many miles yet to go, but you have embarked on the pursuit of an important goal and have made at least some progress toward it.*

- *Note the fact that your initial estimate of the time it would take could easily have been optimistic. If the goal and your methods are still sound and your problem is the rate of progress, then you may still be in good shape. After all, you were wrong about the timetable, not about the goal itself.*

The key question may be how to speed up progress. Often the trade off is between time and money, so consider the following options and implement any that make sense:

- *Borrowing money to finance the endeavor, to live on, or to pay for help or more help*

- *Slowing down progress in order to take on paying work or to address issues that will enable you to speed up later*

- *Scaling back your goals so that you can achieve one or more of them in the near term and show your progress to yourself and others (investors, significant others, etc.)*

- *Getting rid of anything that is slowing down your progress*

Progress, distance, and time are all relative terms. Make an effort to see the progress you have made as well as the distance that remains between you and your goal. Also understand that in many endeavors, progress speeds up as you near the goal.

Get Feedback

What kind of feedback are you getting? By feedback I mean useful judgments from others regarding your endeavor, abilities, and progress. Some of these people may be disinterested or interested observers. Others might be people who can help, especially if they have been there themselves.

Be careful to seek feedback from people who can give you good feedback. Also, listen to the feedback. People understand right away whether you want honest criticism and coaching or whether you just want encouragement. Honest feedback can help you see what you are doing correctly and incorrectly and figure out how to fix things.

Talk with someone objective, a good listener who will ask good questions. Try to find someone who knows you and what you are trying to do, but also speak with people who don't know you and who can just think objectively about what you're doing.

Obsession Isn't Motivation

In common parlance we might say someone is obsessed with something when they spend inordinate amounts of time on it or can't seem to talk about anything else. Don't mistake obsession for motivation. It's different, and it's often not pretty.

It may seem odd that I classify obsession with a lack of motivation. Actually, given the way I defined motivation in Chapter 1—as a desire that's so strong it propels you to act to obtain or achieve the object of your desire—it may seem that obsession is simply an extreme form of motivation. I'd argue that it's not, because the missing element is true desire.

People with clinical obsessions—with obsessive compulsive disorder (OCD)—don't actually want straightened pictures, perfect rows of silverware, clean hands, or five trips around the block before they pull into their driveways. They want relief of the underlying anxiety that drives the behavior. If anything, they want to stop acting on their obsessions.

ob·ses·sion

1. mental, emotional, or behavioral fixation on a person, thing, goal, or activity

2. way of dealing with the world by excluding issues, problems, thoughts and people outside of the area of obsession

But I'm not talking about clinical OCD. I'm just using it to make the point that motivation differs from a healthy pursuit.

Remember back in Chapter 1 when I spoke about being driven as opposed to having drive? People with obsessions are driven. They aren't motivated in the sense that I've been discussing it. For instance, workaholics don't usually stop when they reach their stated goals. They keep working.

work·a·hol·ic

1. a person who works to the exclusion of most other pursuits.

2. a person who may be using work to avoid dealing with other aspects of life.

Striking a Balance

The antidote for obsession is balance in one's life. That's why it's so important to have purposes, goals, and tasks to perform in various areas of your life, not just one. It's hard to do when you're obsessed, but when you hear people pointing out that you're always working or you never have time for anything, try to listen to them.

If you have a hard time listening to them or find their comments upsetting, maybe you are in fact focusing on one area of your life to the exclusion of the others. After all, if there's no truth to it, why would it bother you?

Obsessed, in a Good Way?

Certain artists, entrepreneurs, inventors, and geniuses may be obsessed. They pour all their energy into their work (it's usually work) to create great art, build huge companies, or invent new technologies. If that describes you, maybe you should go with it. But bear in mind—as the divorces, debts, and lawsuits pile up—that not every obsessive is a genius, and vice versa.

Striking a balance doesn't mean achieving a perfectly equal distribution of your energy across all the areas of your life. Sometimes you may have to work harder in one area almost exclusively, for example to establish a business, battle an illness, learn something new, or care for a sick spouse, parent, or child. There's nothing wrong with that, because you can strike the balance later when the big task is completed. It's when you mindlessly pursue one area regardless of real need or progress, and you let the rest of your life go to the dogs, that you should worry about becoming obsessed—and about burnout.

Don't Get Burned

Becoming obsessed, dealing with discouragement, and even simply pushing hard in any area of life can leave a person burned out. I've come close to burnout a few times and in more than one area. To me it's a feeling of being used up, empty,

SIGNS OF BURNOUT

- *Persistent fatigue or exhaustion*

- *Disengagement from things you used to enjoy*

- *Sense of futility or frustration*

- *Constant stress with no end in sight*

unresourceful, and exhausted. It's a lack of ideas, lack of mental and physical energy, and, yes, lack of motivation.

The signs of burnout are well documented. However, one day or one week of symptoms isn't burnout. Look for the duration of symptoms, and of the conditions around you. Burnout is often related to hard work under stressful conditions. Stressful conditions can include inadequate resources, incompetent bosses, financial pressure, production pressure, or people who can't or won't pull their weight. Of course, any fight for survival in the context of illness, prison, or war—any environment of uncertainty or chaos—takes a toll on a person.

As with so many conditions of this type, it's best to avoid burnout rather than to have to cope with it. Since burnout is a perennial topic in our overworked society, you've probably heard about ways to deal with it. Here they are again for easy reference:

- *Take a real, preferably foreign, vacation*

- *Recognize that you can't be all things to everyone at all times*

- Decide what you want out of life, and whether burnout is among those things

- Set aside "sacred" time for the gym, naps, proper meals, walking, sleeping, and other daily rejuvenators; if you think that's impossible, you may be headed for burnout

> When you come to the end of your rope, tie a knot and hang on.
> —Franklin D. Roosevelt (U.S. president)

- Set sharp limits on people who contribute to your stress

Recovering Lost Motivation

Those hints about addressing burnout are also good starting points for recovering lost motivation in general. Here are a number of others:

- If you're discouraged, imagine and accept the worst. That often frees a person to start realistically seeing the possibilities that are short of the worst.

- Dream the dream again. Go back to your original vision and life's purpose. Recall these as vividly as you can and recover that emotional connection you had with them.

○ *Review your goals, plan, and execution. Was everything truly reasonable, or did you get carried away and set unattainable goals or develop an unworkable plan? Did you set reasonable sub-goals? Are the tasks really within your range of skills?*

○ *Consider your options—and choose. Do you need to develop new goals or revamp your plan? Do you need more money or different skills? Where can you access them? Do you need more help?*

Take Action

Keep music or spoken word CDs, books, quotations, prayers, stories, and other items that keep you motivated handy—and use them when you need inspiration. Don't think you don't need them or they won't do any good. You do, and they will.

○ *Go back to the basics. Success in any endeavor depends on diligent application of the basics. But you already know the basics, don't you? Of course you do, but go back and review them anyway. I have repeatedly found that when I go back and reread what I've already learned about writing, editing, business development, communication, relationships, and, yes, motivation, I find new ideas and renewed inspiration.*

○ *Let the action create the mood—and the motivation. Remember, often it's the simple act of taking a few steps that gets you moving, and motivated, again.*

> **TO LEAD PEOPLE, WALK BESIDE THEM**.... WHEN THE BEST LEADER'S WORK IS DONE THE PEOPLE SAY, 'WE DID IT OURSELVES!'
>
> —Lao Tsu (Taoist philosopher)

10

Motivating Others

The extent to which one person can actually motivate another person is open to question. You can persuade people. You can give them incentives. You can guide them in certain directions. You can even inspire them. So if all that adds up to motivation—and it is arguable that it does—you can motivate people.

On the other hand, like the old joke about the psychiatrists changing the lightbulb, people have to want to be motivated. Fortunately, many people do want to be motivated. They want to be called to high purpose, and want someone to ask them to do their best. They want to be part of great undertakings and to help meet the great challenges the human race faces at any given time. The long history of leaders who have motivated employees, students, citizens, soldiers, and athletes to extraordinary feats bears that out—as do other people's responses to those leaders.

In this chapter we look at ways of motivating others, mainly employees, but also in other situations. We'll also revisit or examine for the first time some of the theories about motivating people on the job. As a result, this chapter will help you understand how to motivate others to want to do their best, which is really the best way to motivate them.

Manager or Leader?

I see a manager as someone who understands the role of manager, wants to play that role for his or her employees, and can apply the principles and practices of management on the job. (You can learn more about those principles and practices in *Execution*, another title in this Adams Media series.) Good managers understand their organizations' goals, and the roles that people play in achieving them. They communicate well and can offer guidance, coaching, performance appraisals, and encouragement to their subordinates.

But managers, as well as teachers, coaches, politicians, ministers, and other people in leadership positions, may or may not provide leadership. Frankly, consistent competence in a position is usually all we can ask, and that's hard enough to come by. Leadership demands consistent competence, and more. Essentially, a leader helps people do their best as often as they are

---

MANAGERS

- Understand their role and their subordinates' roles

- Play their role for their subordinates, not for their own aggrandizement

- Know and apply management practices

---

capable of doing it. Leaders understand that only motivated people do their best, and therefore try to motivate people to consistently exert extraordinary effort.

What Motivates? And What Doesn't?

You can look at motivating others in two ways: You can look at it as an exercise in providing rational incentives, and you can look at it in terms of engaging people on a more emotional level and providing emotional payoffs. Notice I said "and" in that sentence. You'll best motivate others if you use a combination of rational incentives and emotional engagement.

Leaders tend to do certain things and have certain things in common. Most of them are good communicators, but it is the way in which they communicate as well as what they communicate. Quite a few of them have a good amount of charisma. They also know what motivates people and they appeal to those things.

cha•ris•ma

1. attractiveness to people based on energy, appearance, and personal magnetism

2. often associated with extraordinary communication skills and charm

3. ability to appeal to people at an emotional, not just intellectual, level

In general, effective leaders:

- *Communicate their purpose and establish the seriousness of that purpose.*

- *Ask people to do things, and set high standards for their performance.*

- *Give people an honest picture of their situation.*

- *Form an emotional bond with their followers.*

Seriousness of Purpose

People are motivated by a sense of purpose. Leaders take the things in their area of responsibility seriously, and convey that seriousness to their followers. They do this in various ways. For instance, if the mission is inherently important—say, it has to do with social justice or helping the unfortunate—they will cite its importance and link it to moral issues, such as fairness and decency. If the mission itself is relatively trivial in the scheme of things—for instance, making auto loans or selling photocopiers—they link the mission to a higher purpose such as professionalism, excellence, service to customers, or responsibilities to shareholders.

Leaders engage their people in the mission and the purpose largely by conveying their conviction that the purpose and mission are worthwhile or, better yet, essential. When a manager honestly believes that the organization's mission is useful, when a teacher believes her subject is exciting, or when a politician believes his cause is just, they convey that belief to people, and most people want something to believe in.

Asking People to Act and Setting High Standards

Leaders typically not only ask people to do things, but also challenge them to do their best. This creates an atmosphere of high motivation because you can do your best only when you're highly motivated. Moreover, the leader is watching. He or she wants you to do your best and cares whether or not you do your best. As a result, you care about doing your best.

The most motivating activity is one that engages people because it is challenging enough to test them while also being achievable. Effective leaders realize that most of us are not doing our best at all times. They therefore challenge us to do our best, by setting high standards and enforcing those standards. They have the moral authority to do this because they have already established that the mission and purpose are serious.

The fact is that some people are not interested in doing their best or are not interested in serving a certain purpose. The leader creates an environment in which those people either opt out of the organization (or the classroom, or the movement) or are forced out by peer pressure.

> Management means helping people to get the best out of themselves, not organizing things.
>
> **—Lauren Appley (motivational coach)**

Painting an Honest Picture

It's no coincidence that so many would-be leaders are scuttled when they are caught in lies. It's not that people expect leaders to be perfect. It's that they expect them to be honest, at least in their areas of official responsibility. They definitely expect them to convey an honest picture of the situation they face.

The basic element here is trust. People put themselves in the hands of the leader. They turn over a measure of their self-directedness to the leader, by allowing the leader to direct them. (I'm discussing actual leaders, not dictators who rule by force.) To do that, the followers must trust the leader. If the leader proves unworthy of that trust, then he undermines the entire leader-follower relationship, and people's motivation.

Take Action

Browse *www.motivational central.com* for thoughts, information, and quotes on motivation.

Leaders have to give people an honest picture of the situation not only to maintain trust, but also so people know where they are in the mission, what they must do, and why they must do it. Leaders must be honest or people are operating on false information, which is not only unfair to them but also undercuts their effectiveness. Falsehoods inevitably come out and when they do, the followers feel betrayed and unmotivated.

Forging Emotional Bonds

Remember that motivation is a feeling and a decision. People agree to follow a leader at least partly on the basis of the emotional bond they feel with him or her. The leader's call to be of service to an important purpose generates the enthusiasm, energy, effort, and dedication that characterize motivation.

> Leadership is the art of getting someone else to do something you want done because he wants to do it.
> —**Dwight D. Eisenhower (U.S. general and president)**

These emotions also foster team spirit and group effort. A team or organization coalesces around the leader. The team members bond with one another as well as with the leader. The leader knows this and uses team spirit—the group response to the call to excellence and the collective standard of high performance—in pursuit of the goal.

The Importance of Congruence

In a way, leaders cast a spell over people. I don't mean in some mystical sense. I mean that they engage the followers emotionally so that the followers' emotions override logical objections and lesser emotions. For instance, an inspiring leader can enable people to forget that the mission has a low chance of success, that their resources are strained, and that they are totally exhausted. The emotional bond with the leader and enthusiastic engagement in the mission overrides those things.

But what happens when the spell is broken? What happens when we see our politicians giving taxpayer dollars to their campaign contributors; when religious leaders not only commit crimes and sins but also try to cover them up; and when executives grab the lion's share of the rewards for an organization's success? People lose their motivation to follow the leader and to work for the purpose.

To motivate others, a leader must present a congruent picture to his or her followers. Why? Because if the leader doesn't take the purpose and goals seriously, then neither will the followers. If the leader sets high standards for others, but doesn't apply them to himself, then neither will the followers apply them. The leader must at least try to live up to the idealized version of himself that he helps people create—at least within the arena in which he leads them—or the emotional bond between leader and follower will dissolve.

About Employee Motivation

Haw • thorne ef • fect

1. improvement in an area of employee performance when management focuses on it

2. effect of researchers' attention on human subjects

The study of employee motivation began in earnest with studies conducted in the 1920s and 1930s at a Western Electric Company site known as the Hawthorne plant. In this study of productivity, researchers found that workers became motivated to produce more simply because they knew they were in a study. This phenomenon, called the Hawthorne effect, basically states that when management focuses on something, that thing starts to improve. Unfortunately, the Hawthorne effect is almost always temporary. It does, however, underscore the importance of management attention to employees.

First, let's just be clear about the behaviors we want to motivate employees to perform. In general, managers want employees to:

- ○ Support the organization's values, mission, and goals

- ○ Use productive, effective, and efficient work practices

- ○ Deliver quality products and services to customers

- ○ Cooperate with coworkers, other departments, suppliers, and stakeholders

- ○ Minimize wasted time, materials, and costs

- ○ Remain with the organization as long as their services are required

- ○ Represent the organization in positive ways in their communities

Motivators of Positive Employee Behavior

There are many things managers can do to motivate positive employee behavior. Here are the twelve most important ones:

1. Present clear goals, standards, expectations, and deadlines
2. Assign challenging but achievable goals
3. Provide adequate training, support, and coaching
4. Ask employees for their input on assignments and decisions
5. Allow employees to determine their working methods to the extent possible
6. Explain decisions and how and why they have been made, and that employee support for decisions is expected once they are made
7. Reward good and extraordinary performance with good and extraordinary pay
8. Provide competitive benefits and working conditions
9. Give employees regular informal feedback on their performance and periodic formal, written evaluations
10. Model the desired behaviors and prohibit rude, prejudiced, sexist, or unfair speech or behavior
11. Recognize that employees have personal lives as well as professional lives
12. Maintain and express a sense of humor and humanity

To the employee, the manager is the organization. Thus, the relationship a superior forges with subordinates largely determines the subordinates' motivation. This is the case for managers as well as for leaders.

Motivators of Negative Employee Behavior

Negative employee behavior usually takes the form of undermining the organization or petty theft. By undermining, I mean slacking off; doing substandard work; cutting corners; complaining; treating customers, suppliers, or coworkers badly; being chronically absent or late; and insubordination. By petty theft, I mean stealing small items of company property and using company time or resources for non-company purposes. I am leaving aside the violent behavior of disturbed employees, problems of drug and alcohol abuse, and serious crimes such as embezzlement, fraud, and grand larceny.

What motivates normal people and formerly solid employees to undermine a company or engage in petty theft? Usually, it is some real or perceived form of unfairness on the part of management. When certain workers feel exploited or inadequately compensated, they can justify negative or even dishonest behavior. Under pressure to achieve aggressive sales or profit goals, management may even encourage or condone dishonest sales or accounting practices. If so, then those managers run the risk of encouraging dishonest practices against the company, as well as the risk of termination and jail.

Take Action

Many executives and entrepreneurs learn about leadership by reading biographies of great leaders. Among the most popular with business people are William Manchester's *The Last Lion*, on Winston Churchill (1983), and *American Caesar*, on General Douglas MacArthur (1978).

When employees are undermining the organization, management has to ask what may be motivating that behavior. Most people want to do a good job and want the rewards that go with that. Most employees are not out to sabotage their employers. So, management should first see that the basic motivators are in place, then look at themselves.

Back to Management

Okay, let's turn from leadership back to plain old management. What have the researchers of on-the-job motivation learned about motivating people in the workplace?

Here are the key lessons:

Hygiene factors are not motivators. Much of what companies often see as goodies for employees, such as pay, benefits, and good working conditions, are hygiene factors. (You'll recall the discussion of hygiene factors in Chapter 2, and that according to Frederick Herzberg, employees are not motivated by them.)

Competent management is a hygiene factor. Employees see competent managers—those who can set goals, coach people to achieve them, communicate and enforce standards, and follow up to see that tasks are completed and people are rewarded—as something they deserve (and they are correct). Companies that leave incompetent managers in place do themselves a real disservice.

Managers, professionals, and knowledge workers respond well to what Herzberg calls "Motivators." These Motivators include job content, professional challenges, and feelings of mission, belonging, affiliation, and achievement. Also, many people are motivated by control over their job content and time and by the opportunity to strike a balance between their work and personal lives. The chance to develop professional and personal skills motivates most people as well. People want to avoid boredom and continue to grow. Those things occur through increasingly challenging assignments, rotation through various areas of the organization, and formal training, development, and mentoring.

There are many ways to reduce workers' motivation. Employees find various aspects of organizational life demotivating, and these are often things that management could change without spending a cent. One huge problem is office politics—the kind that drives decisions that are incongruent with the organization's stated goals. Other problems include lack of communication, lack of information about the business, lack of transparency (or even logic) in the way management makes decisions, and persistent, unsolved problems.

Workers at every level want attention and recognition. Employees find attention and recognition motivating. They want to feel valued and it's up to their managers to make them feel that way. People want to be included, informed, and asked for their opinions. It's also just good management to ask employees for their opinions, given that they know how effectively they are doing their work.

So, You Want to Be a Manager

People often take on roles for the wrong reasons or without understanding the real nature of the commitment. This happens a lot with the role of manager. Many people want to be managers because they like the idea of earning more money, having people report to them, sitting in the corner office, and going to lunch with the CEO. But many of these folks actually have very little interest in playing the role of manager for their employees. They have little interest in setting goals, delegating tasks, correcting mistakes, appraising performance, and so on.

In other words, they want to play the role of manager not for their employees, but for themselves. They're not interested in what they can bring to the role, but in what they can take from it. They're not interested in supporting the company's purpose, but in having the company support their purpose. Their purpose is to get, not give. They're not taking the role of manager for what they can put into it, but for what they can get out of it. These are the managers who expect employees to suck up to them, bolster their egos, and make them look good.

So, as with any role, if you want to be a manager mainly for yourself or for what you can get out of it, think twice about taking that promotion. If on the other hand, you want the role for what you can bring to it, for what you can do for the organization and your subordinates, then you may have a good match.

Everyone Is Different

While people share many basic needs, they go about getting them met in various ways. Also, some people feel some needs more intensely than they do others. For instance, inner-directed people tend to do things themselves and must be encouraged to ask for help. They have to understand that they aren't helping the outfit when they work on a problem for days because they find it intellectually stimulating, when Charlie over there could have solved it in one hour. They are also often motivated by their own internal standards more than the organization's standards.

When they're working in organizations, inner-directed people must understand that while they have their own internal standards, the organization may need work of a lower, higher, or different standard. If someone spends two weeks working on a project that met the organization's (and client's) standards a week ago, they just wasted a week. Inner-directed people need to know that the organization values their contribution, but that their contribution must meet the organization's needs.

Similarly, outer-directed people are motivated by recognition and by being part of a team. At times their social needs—say for constant feedback, conversations, or long meetings—can distract others and throw things off course. They may enjoy discussing the many potential ways of doing something more than getting it done. Their need for approval can hobble their ability to make decisions and to work independently. They may even try to avoid responsibility or accountability for a task or result.

Outer-directed people must learn how to work on their own when necessary, and to take responsibility for their work. They must realize that while they find interaction motivating, interaction must move the team toward its goals.

knowl•edge work

1. work performed by educated people producing research, software, consulting, media content, and laws and regulations

2. work performed in companies in financial services, advertising, media, and consulting and in government and academia

Wanted: Real Leaders

Leadership is becoming essential in business because many companies now employ mainly well-educated people engaged in knowledge work. This kind of work demands motivation, creativity, and flexibility, and you cannot simply ask (let alone order) people to be motivated, creative, and flexible.

Leadership has also come to the fore because most companies have moved away from so-called command-and-control

management. Command-and-control management characterizes manufacturing environments and organizations staffed largely by lower skill workers who can produce their work according to strict procedures and "traditional" management.

While a traditional manager directs people to do what they should do, a leader gets people to do what they should do and more with less direction and greater efficiency. Leaders do this mainly by communicating the overall result the organization aims to produce and by motivating people to produce at very high standards of quality.

"

WITH **ORDINARY TALENT AND EXTRAORDINARY PERSEVERANCE**, ALL THINGS ARE ATTAINABLE.

"

—Thomas Foxwell Buxton
(British politician)

11 The Motivational Toolbox

Many of the things discussed in this book—purpose, goals, theories, and so on—operate at a fairly high level. That's because the work of motivating yourself mainly comes down to deciding what you want and then deciding to pursue it. Once you make those high-level decisions, a lot of the work of motivating yourself is done.

But not all of it. There are, even in the most motivated people, moments of doubt, drift, indecision, and plain laziness. I'm not talking about lost motivation as I did in Chapter 9. That occurs at a different level and requires a more strategic response.

No, here I'm talking about things that you can do to get motivated and stay motivated at a tactical level. I'm talking about things you can use to motivate yourself to take action on a consistent, daily basis. These are what I would call tools of motivation, because you can use them on yourself to get jump-started, to inspire yourself, or to boost your energy and enthusiasm.

Write Your Own Obituary

A number of authors have recommended that you sit down and write your own obituary, and I'm going to join them. I've done it, and I found it quite motivating. It's an exercise in constructing your ideal life.

The key to getting something from the exercise is to be completely honest with yourself. Don't say you founded an order of contemplative nuns if you really want to found a school for aspiring comedians. Of course, you can write whatever you want and then edit it for honesty later.

This exercise helped me realize that I was wasting my time in corporate life. Not only would I be happier if I figured out how to make a living by writing books, but so would my employers. So that's what I did.

The Major Project

I've asked you to think big. Small goals just aren't that motivating to most of us. Of course, you'll recall that major goals break down into small ones and into tasks. That's fine, because those smaller goals and tasks are in service of the larger goal.

On the other hand, every endeavor has grunt work and difficulties associated with it. The test of your motivation in an area is whether or not you view the grunt work and difficulties as part of the deal, or as showstoppers.

For instance, actors have to go on auditions; most of them hate it, but they love acting so they deal with it. Salespeople hate cold calls but they make them

The Wisdom of the Donald

Real estate magnate Donald Trump once said it's easier to sell million-dollar condos in Manhattan than it is to collect rents in Queens. He's saying that whatever you do, you're going to be working anyway—so why not work in an area where the rewards are bigger, and perhaps even easier to come by? It's a matter of scale, and, if nothing else, Trump operates on a grand scale.

because a few cold calls will result in sales calls and they love selling. Writers hate getting rejection slips when they send out articles and manuscripts; but we do it because we love getting published.

Whatever you want to do will have at least some drudge work and problems that you actually dislike dealing with. Make the decision to deal with it, and accept that as part of the price you'll pay to do what you really want to do.

Tell People, or Don't

Some people find that making a big announcement to one and all—"I'm going to run the New York Marathon (or write a screenplay that will get me an agent, or lose thirty pounds by June 30th)"—motivating. Or they make a smaller announcement to a limited group of trusted individuals, or one individual. They find that the possibility of a public or semi-private failure to be motivating.

171

Other people like to work on their training, screenplay, or diet in private, with an audience of one. It's not just that they dislike the possibility of public failure, but that they enjoy the idea of surprising people on the day when they join the marathon runners, the screenwriters, or the few among us who can wear a Speedo or thong without bumming everyone out.

Managing your motivation calls for making the right call. I myself like the secretive approach, because failure in my own eyes—when it happens—is painful enough, and I love surprising people.

Harness and Redirect Anger

If you're prone to anger in any of its many forms—rage, blame, self-destructiveness, or vengeance—try using it as motivation instead. This means directing the anger into a useful channel. Rage won't help, except perhaps by letting you blow off steam. Blame, as I've mentioned, can lead you to misunderstand the problem or dump on yourself. Speaking of dumping on yourself, self-destructive behavior will only set you back in various ways, and may shorten your life. Vengeance won't help either, and can definitely hurt your reputation.

However, you can channel the emotion of anger—or rather, its energy—into useful venues. For instance, I've been able to seek "revenge" by diving into a problem, tearing it apart, and improving my skills or working methods. Anger has often helped me work harder.

Many people have found real motivation in the urge to "show the SOBs a thing or two." Of course, the SOBs in question are rarely aware of your existence, and even if they are, they're not thinking about you. As I said, motivation is as much a mind game as it is anything else. So make a game of using your anger to propel yourself in productive directions.

> The best revenge is massive success.
> —Frank Sinatra
> (singer and actor)

Make a Commitment to Yourself

I've often been struck by the fact that we will often do all sorts of things for employers, professors, parents, children, and various "authorities," but not for ourselves. If you can put out extraordinary effort for everyone but yourself, you have to start asking yourself why that is.

Generally, we do for others because we have made a commitment to them. We make a lot of commitments like that, and then start to feel overcommitted. So, when it comes time to make a commitment to ourselves, we don't.

However, unless you make a commitment to yourself—to do the things that are important to you—you may never get to those things. Sadly, few of the people you are committed to are going to ask you to stop and make a commitment to yourself. And that's fine, because only you can make a commitment to yourself.

173

Try These Tools

Here are four standard tools that people use to motivate themselves. Not every one of them works for everyone, and many people (like me) use various tools at various times for various goals and tasks. Try the ones that appeal to you but, again, give them a chance to work.

Visualization: Mental visualization is among the most popular and powerful motivational tools. There's really no right or wrong way to do it, but people tend to get the best results by relaxing with deep breathing and then creating vivid, very detailed mental images of the things they'll do and the results they'll achieve. Visualization has proven particularly useful in competitive sports and other physical activities.

Positive Self-Talk: Okay, I admit it, I talk to myself. Always have, always will. I find it hard to believe that everyone doesn't. But everyone does have a running dialogue in their heads. It's incredibly important that you not only refrain from dumping on yourself, but also make that internal dialogue as positive as you can without crossing the line into insanity.

Look Up, Stand Up, and Smile: Anthony Robbins recommends these techniques, and I've tried them and found them to be effective. Robbins is

Listen Up!

I find it impossible to listen to certain pop songs and feel down. Among the dozens are "Walk of Life" (Dire Straits), "Sexbomb" (Tom Jones), "Girls Just Want to Have Fun" (Cyndi Lauper), "Holiday" (Madonna), "Superfreak" (Rick James), and, of course, "Hey Ya!" (OutKast). Yes, some of these tunes are inane, and that's the point! Make your own list.

very good at examining how people appear when they are unmotivated, and getting them to do the opposite. For instance, unmotivated people look down at the ground, slump, shuffle, and frown. He recommends looking up, standing up straight, putting some spring in your step, and smiling. Like I said, it works for me. It's extremely hard to smile and still feel down. If you feel a bit like an idiot, go with that. You'd be a bigger idiot to ruin your day with sadness.

The Buddy System: Many people find it motivating to enlist a friend in certain projects, such as working out, building a business, making home improvements, traveling, or meeting members of the opposite gender. Not only do you get to share the joys and heartaches, but also the knowledge and techniques. When one of you doesn't feel like it, the other can provide encouragement.

Middle Passages

At the start of a book I feel a real burst of enthusiasm, and then another shot of energy toward the end as the finish line comes into view. I've come to expect a saggy feeling in the middle of a large project. I view this as part of the process rather than boredom, doubt, or failure to master the material.

Anticipate Down Cycles

It is totally natural for energy to flag and for enthusiasm to fade, but that does not affect your basic motivation, which runs much deeper. It resides at the level of deeply considered decisions and serious commitments to your purpose and goals.

Energy and enthusiasm run in cyclical patterns. Highs are called highs because they stand in contrast to lows. If you understand that you cannot run full-throttle all the time, and that setbacks will occur and that they will temporarily diminish your mood, then you will expect it.

In any area, seasoned professionals know how to observe themselves dispassionately. You may feel listless, unenthusiastic or even bored, but these aren't problems or setbacks. They are just a natural part of the motivational cycle.

Simply Endure

At times, we find ourselves in situations that we must simply endure. Sometimes it's a mess created by our own blunders, by responsibilities we have accepted and perhaps shouldn't have, or by horrible twists of fate. Where do you get the motivation to keep on going?

I believe that there are times when you just have to avoid thinking about either quitting or going on. You simply have to endure. There's a moment in the TV miniseries of James Clavell's terrific novel *Shogun* that has always stuck with me. A Christian missionary is attempting to convert a Japanese man who is mightily resisting his efforts. At a point of total frustration, the missionary yells, "Do you want to spend all of eternity burning in hell?" to which the Japanese man replies, "If that is my karma, I will endure it."

Having been reared in the Christian faith, I found that reply remarkable, even from a fictional character. Here is a fellow with so much faith in his ability to endure that he believes that if eternal damnation is his fate, he will find a way to deal with it.

I and people I know have endured times of trouble simply by going on. You may be out of tears, out of prayers, and out of hope, but you can still—perhaps out of sheer stubbornness—keep going.

> **kar•ma**
>
> 1. concept in Buddhism and Hinduism that people's actions in this life will affect their future fate, particularly once they've been reincarnated
>
> 2. more broadly, the future effect of past and current actions, as in "stealing creates bad karma"

When you're enduring something, try to notice the small pleasures, occasional humor, and people's kindness. Those things are there even when you have fallen apart.

Start—and Regain— a Virtuous Cycle

When you take action to pursue something that's important to you, you ignite a virtuous cycle in which the very act of acting encourages you to act. When you get results, the motivation increases. But the world rewards our efforts with what B. F. Skinner (whom you met in Chapter 2) called intermittent reinforcement. Our efforts don't always reward us in the ways we would prefer.

That's why the phrase "You can't win them all" was coined. The problem is that when you do lose, you can lose momentum and even motivation. Somewhat contrary to Skinner's thinking, many of us are totally fine with systems of continuous reward. It's when the rewards stop that we lose motivation.

Many of us have seen the virtuous cycle broken when we've given in to temptation during a program of change. For instance, one missed session at the gym turns into two, and two turns into two weeks. One

> **vi·cious cy·cle or vir·tu·ous cy·cle**
>
> 1. pattern of behavior in which negative or positive behavior reinforces itself
>
> 2. related to B. F. Skinner's concept of reinforcement, but also to the simple idea of habit

doughnut becomes a box of doughnuts, or one cigarette becomes a pack.

Why is that?

It's because the "rewards" of a vicious cycle quickly replace those of a virtuous cycle. We start believing

that we can't do it because of one screw-up. We think our motivation is gone because we lost it for a day. We start thinking that we can't change, that maybe we don't even want to change, and that we should just learn to love our fat selves, or our smoking selves, or whatever.

This is why they say if you get thrown by a horse, you should get right back on. It's not to show the horse who's boss—it's to show yourself who's boss. If you fall off your motivational horse and miss a day or a week at the gym, or smoke a cigarette or a pack, you must get back on that horse and put the slip-up behind you. You may not feel motivated to do so, but you have to. In a matter of a few days you will re-establish the virtuous cycle—and regain your motivation.

Be a Professional

Craftsmen and artists have a motivation to do good work that transcends their paychecks. They have standards based upon the tradition of the craft, work of previous practitioners, and principles and practices

The Code of the Professional

The traditional professions are medicine, law, accounting, and architecture. They require advanced study and licensing and have codes of ethics and conduct. Those codes motivate practitioners to take pride in their work in ways that go beyond money and customer service. For instance, the customer may always be right, but the client isn't. It's a professional's job to tell the client when he's wrong.

developed over time. They generally love the work itself, and often find that their real challenge in life is finding a way to get paid for it.

For instance, there are people who still make and sell wooden pleasure boats on the coast of Maine, the Great Lakes area, and in the Pacific Northwest. The boats are far more expensive than comparable fiberglass craft. But there are people who can and will pay for that level of craftsmanship. The boat-builders are not getting rich, because it takes months to build one and even the thousands of dollars they receive for a small boat doesn't add up to a great hourly rate. They do the work because they love doing it, and because they love the result.

When I lived in Brooklyn, I owned a car with an unusual problem. Every now and then, the electrical system would totally cut out while I was driving, a disconcerting situation. It was a short circuit, the location of which stumped the mechanics at two different shops. A mechanic at a third shop insisted that he could find the short. He asked me to leave the car with him and to let him drive it for a while. It took him three days, but he finally found it in the wiring in the right front fender behind the headlight. And he fixed it.

I patronized that mechanic until I moved to New England, because he saw finding that short as a professional challenge. You can't put that kind of motivation into someone by paying them. They either have that sense of professional pride, or they don't.

Say What You Mean

Our motivation becomes tainted, skewed, and diverted when we don't say what we think. We've all heard a lot of talk about being true to yourself, but that can be a deep, abstract, philosophical idea or a greeting card sentiment.

The real question is, how do you go about being true to yourself?

Here's how to start: Call 'em like you see 'em. Don't say yes when you mean no. Don't say yes or no when you mean maybe. And don't be afraid to say "I don't know."

One way we get into real motivational trouble is when we agree to do certain things, by a certain time or in a certain way that we don't really agree with, and hope that somehow things will work out. Why do we do this?

Well, sometimes it can't be helped. If you work for a boss who's making unreasonable demands, you may have to agree with them—for now. If you work as an independent contractor and need the money, you may take on work that you shouldn't take on or agree to a deadline that you can't really meet.

Those are situations we all want to avoid, but sometimes we can't. So, the longer-term motivational issue is to develop enough options or enough power so that you don't have to agree to something when you disagree. The shorter-term motivational issue is to understand at the outset that you agreed to something disagreeable, for good reasons, and you now have to live with that. You bite the bullet, tough it out, and use the short-term pain to motivate yourself to develop the right long-term situation.

The Sad and Happy Truth

Motivation is a wonderful thing, but at one level— leaving aside all of the mind games, goals, tools, quotes, and, for that matter, books—you either have it or you don't.

By that I don't mean that you are either a motivated person or you're not. I mean that you have either discovered or decided what you really want to do, or you haven't, and you are either doing that thing, or not.

In other words, if you find you have to spend a lot of time and effort motivating yourself to do something, you're probably not doing something that you really want to do. The people who I've seen achieve the most success have achieved it mainly by doing something that they already felt motivated to do, not by motivating themselves to do something they basically didn't want to do. I have seen the most success in my own life when I've been doing something that I really wanted to do, rather than motivating myself to do something that I didn't want to be doing.

> In three words I can sum up everything I have learned about life: It goes on.
> —Robert Frost (poet)

So, it's quite simple, but rarely easy: Discover or decide what you really want to do—what you find valuable, enjoyable, challenging, and worthwhile—and go do that. And you'll never have to think much about motivation again.